Papagena

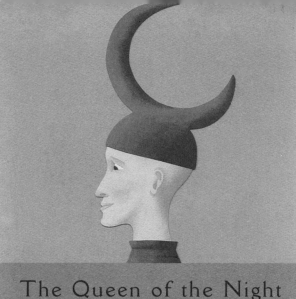

The Queen of the Night

First Priest

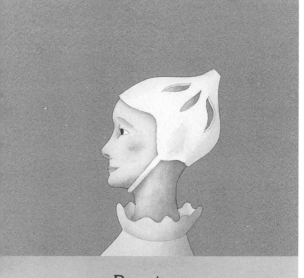

Pamina

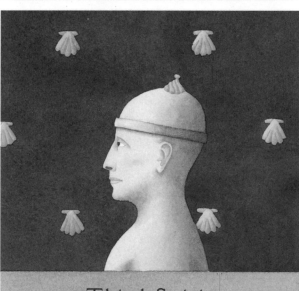

Third Spirit

Third Lady

Second Priest

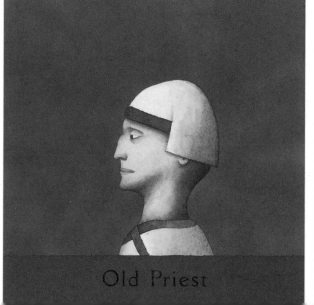

Old Priest

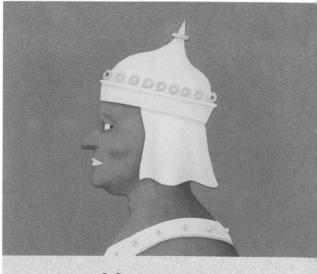

Monostatos

The
Magic
Flute

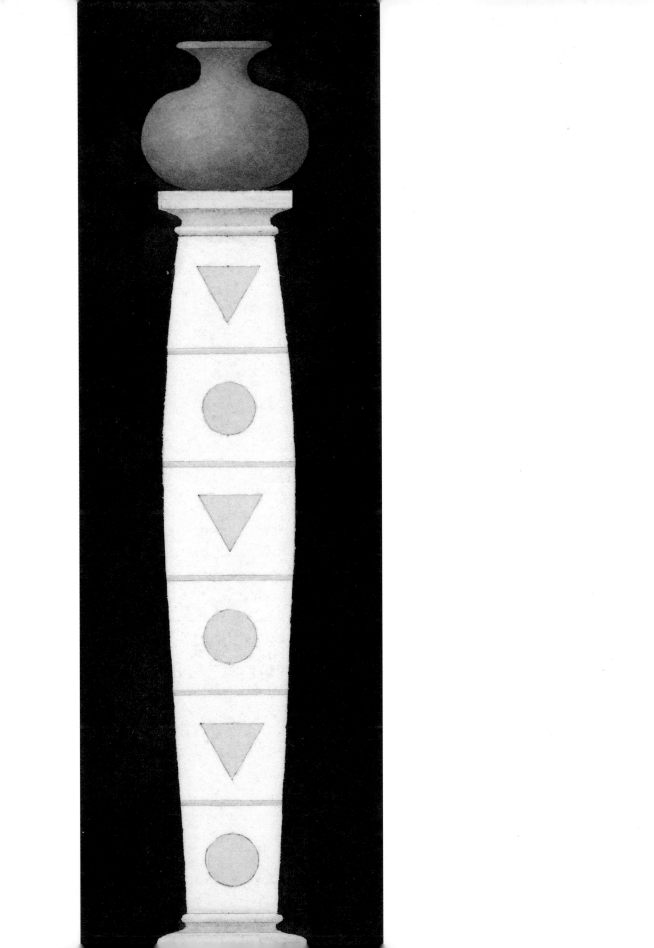

Music by
WOLFGANG AMADEUS MOZART

Libretto by
EMANUEL SCHIKANEDER

The Magic Flute

Davide Pizzigoni

Translation and Introduction by
J. D. McCLATCHY

ABBEVILLE PRESS PUBLISHERS
New York London Paris

CONTENTS

ACT ONE

ACT TWO

INTRODUCTION

J. D. McClatchy

Since its very first performance, on September 30, 1791, *The Magic Flute (Die Zauberflöte)* has been both popular and esteemed. The opera was an instant success with its first audiences. All of Mozart's earlier operas had been written for gilded court theaters filled with polite, bewigged aristocrats. *The Magic Flute,* on the other hand, was written for a commercial theater used to staging farces and operettas, rigged with stage machinery to make spectacular effects, and thronged with the common people. And that has been its home ever since, around the world. For more than two centuries now, its unique combination of the sublime and the ridiculous has worked its theatrical magic. Farce and symbolism, fairy-tale adventures and obscure Masonic lore succeed one another in a dizzying sequence that never fails to convince and captivate. As it has from the start, the opera enchants both the novice and the sophisticate, the child and the connoisseur.

One of the first children to see the opera was Mozart's seven-year-old son, Karl. Mozart himself had conducted the opera's first three performances, and once free of musical duties he would return to the theater as a member of the audience to bask in the astonished applause. He took young Karl to one of those early performances and wrote to his wife that the boy was "absolutely delighted." Three years later, no less a figure than Goethe, enthralled by the music's sublimity and compassion, had it performed at the court theater in Weimar and began a sequel to it. Even the dour and lofty Beethoven later claimed that "Mozart's greatest work remains *The Magic Flute.*" It can truly be said that no opera has a more universal appeal, transcending age and experience, language and class, than does *The Magic Flute.*

For all the joy it has given, for all the praise it lavishes on reason and devotion, the opera emerged from a dark period in Mozart's own life. In 1790 he was thirty-four and had been famous since he was a child, performing for crowned heads. But as a composer dependent on the whims of patrons, he sometimes found it difficult to make an adequate living for himself and his family. Opera was his passion, but his earlier successes—*The Marriage of Figaro* in 1786, *Don Giovanni* in 1787, and *Così fan Tutte* in January 1790—had led to no permanent position. Instead, as he wrote to a friend in the spring of 1790, "for some time you must have noticed my constant sadness." Though he had been touring constantly as a performer, accepting every commission, and working at a frantic pace, his debts still mounted. Conservative critics complained of the capricious challenges his music posed, and his ambitions ran ahead of the expectations of listeners. There were cracks in his marriage. To his acquaintances, he began to seem alternately eccentric and despondent, withdrawn into a private world. "If people could see into my heart," he wrote, "I should almost feel ashamed. To me everything is cold—cold as ice. . . . Everything seems empty." Worst of all, by the beginning of 1791 his inspiration was running dry. Just as he seemed to be drifting into a dark silence, a spark was lit.

Mozart had met Emanuel Schikaneder (1751–1812) in Salzburg a decade earlier, when Schikaneder's troupe of players played a season in the city. They performed

Shakespeare and Goldoni, ballets and melodramas, as well as the *Singspiel,* or drama-with-music. Mozart adored the theater and often composed incidental music for plays. He and Schikaneder became fast friends, attended each other's performances, played skittles and went on shooting parties together. When Mozart left for Munich, Schikaneder was seen running after the coach to say good-bye. Ten years later, in May 1791, they renewed their friendship in Vienna, where Schikaneder was running the Theater auf der Wieden. He too was in financial trouble and asked Mozart to collaborate on a new project he hoped would take advantage of the public's taste for *Zauberopern,* magic operas based on mythological tales and packed with preposterous turns of events and improbable stage effects. Mozart hesitated at first, but by July he had completed the first of the opera's two acts. Schikaneder had lent him a small wooden summerhouse in the garden adjoining the theater, and it is there that Mozart wrote the rest of *The Magic Flute.* His work was interrupted by two new commissions—a mysterious one for a requiem that eventually came to haunt him, and the other for *La Clemenza di Tito,* an opera to celebrate the coronation in Prague of Leopold II as King of Bohemia, written in just eighteen days. He returned to Vienna in September, with a few parts of *The Magic Flute* left to complete. On September 28, he finished the March of the Priests for Act Two, and on the 29th he wrote the Overture—just in time for the premiere the next day. Schikaneder himself played Papageno, and Mozart's sister-in-law, Josepha Hofer, sang the role of Queen of the Night. Mozart was in the pit, conducting from the harpsichord. By the time the lights came up, the audience—after having insisted that several arias be repeated—was on its feet, cheering.

Both Mozart and Schikaneder were Masons. The confraternity of Freemasonry was an important part of the eighteenth-century Enlightenment, its members promoting the cause of rationality and reform. Mozart must have approved of the group's hatred of hierarchy, its idealistic teachings based on equality and tolerance, its espousal of salvation through reason and brotherly love. In Vienna, he was admitted to the "Beneficence" Lodge in December 1784. The speaker at his induction ceremony addressed him in these words: "Favorite of a guardian angel. Friend of the sweetest muse. Chosen by benevolent Nature to move our hearts through rare magical powers and to pour consolation and comfort into our souls. You shall be embraced by all the warm feelings of mankind, which you so wonderfully express through your fingers, through which stream all the magnificent works of your ardent imagination!" Shortly afterward, Mozart was promoted to the highest rank, that of Master Mason, and he was a loyal and active member until his death. Masonic rites—the padlock, the silence, the priesthood, its initiatory rites of passage—must have appealed to the composer, who was fascinated all his life by codes and tests. The secret rituals are part of *The Magic Flute*'s structure, and the Masonic vision—embodied in Sarastro, the ideal, benevolent Father, the Great Architect of the common good—is at the opera's heart.

Some years after Mozart's death, his sister Marianne wrote down her memories of their childhood together. His rich fantasy life was apparent from the start:

> He would think out a kingdom for himself as we traveled from one place to another, and this he called the Kingdom of Back *[das Königreich Rücken]* —why this name, I can no longer recall. This kingdom and its inhabitants were endowed with everything that could make them good and happy children. He was the king of this land—and this notion became so rooted within him, and he carried it so far, that our servant, who could draw a little, had to make a chart of it, and he would dictate the names of the cities, market towns, and villages to him.

This is the Mozart whose imagination was fired by the plot of *The Magic Flute,* the Mozart who never lost his sense of play and wonder. There are readers who will see in Tamino's search for and submission to the mighty Sarastro a wish-fulfillment fantasy of Mozart's own troubled relationship with his father, Leopold. Or view Papageno's happily fallen humanity as a version of Mozart's darker, lustful impulses. Other commentators have wanted historical allegory, with the Queen of the Night a satiric picture of the autocratic Austrian empress Maria Theresa, and Sarastro an homage to her successor, the tolerant Joseph II. But the opera's triumph has less to do with psychobiography or history than with the universal story of a hero's quest for his true home, a home made up of both memory and desire.

Schikaneder's libretto has often been derided. Some have disliked its mix of high and low, or criticized the story as a muddle that switches its emphasis halfway through. One critic went so far as to call it "one of the most absurd specimens of that form of literature in which absurdity is regarded as a matter of course." Yet no audience has ever had trouble following the story or failed to be moved by it. The reason, of course, is that beyond the tangled plot, beyond the high jinks and stock characters, there exists a deeper psychological and emotional drama. Schikaneder drew his libretto from two main sources. Its more serious Masonic aspect derives from Abbé Jean Terrason's utopian *Séthos* (1731); its fairy-tale quest draws on A. J. Liebeskind's story "Lulu, oder die Zauberflöte," collected in Christoph Martin Wieland's *Dschinnistan* (1789).

There are aspects of Schikaneder's pastiche that merit special notice. No woman would ever have been admitted to the inner sanctum, much less the membership, of any Masonic lodge the way Pamina is accepted along with Tamino into Sarastro's temple. In fact, it is Pamina who leads the way through the trials by fire and water; her unquestioning devotion and bravery—like that of later operatic heroines, from Beethoven's Leonora to Wagner's Brünnhilde—are as much the portrait of perfection in action as the picture of her first given to Tamino is the portrait of beauty itself. The portrait of Pamina that so moves Tamino cannot speak, nor is Tamino allowed to speak as part of his initiation. It is ironic that silence is used so expressively in a work overflowing with musical genius. It is music that finally speaks of the pair's love, of their victory over darkness and deceit.

Through the opera's folkloric charm continually swirl undercurrents of myth. The magic flute itself, with its ability to render wild beasts spellbound, is a version of Orpheus's lyre. And like Orpheus, Tamino and his creators are rescuers. In the end, music rescues and reconciles: all tricks and reversals are undone, all true desires brought to light in the opera's final resplendent chorus. And all along, Mozart finds in the exotic or the farcical the outlines of the ideal and the haunts of the heart.

Artists from Karl Friedrich Schinkel and Simon Quaglio in the early nineteenth century to Marc Chagall and David Hockney more recently have created ingenious designs for *The Magic Flute.* And now the opera has been staged again in Davide Pizzigoni's vividly theatrical imagination. Whimsy and wisdom both are featured in the paintbox-bright colors of his pages. That the characters come to be wittily identified by their shoes is entirely appropriate for an opera that opens with a prince fleeing a monster and that follows the quest of Tamino to rescue his beloved and of Pamina to escape her captors. Pizzigoni's collages and cutouts are little dream-theaters. Motifs—column and crescent, shell and bird and blossom—recur, and a side drapery of clouds or mountains or trees continually reminds us that the curtains of consciousness have parted on a tale made out of symbols and suggestions. Central to both dream-work and this opera is the magic of transformation, and the artist's hand here is continually at work: buttons are fastened to the night sky and suddenly changed to stars; sharp arrow tips are plumped to become hearts.

In larger ways, too, the story's strange weave is interpreted by clever and unexpected connections. Traditionally, the Three Ladies have brandished silver spears to slay the evil serpent. But here Pizzigoni portrays them as wielding red roses feathered like arrows. And when later we see the magic flute itself, it too is red and in flower—and the link between sources of power is delicately made. Page-high faces keep us focused on the characters themselves at moments of crisis or intimacy, but Pizzigoni also pulls back to abstract spaces—the vast empty rooms of palace or forest or temple, the long perspectives in which the characters undergo their journeys. In this, his work resembles what Wolfgang Hildesheimer says is the essence of Mozart's own art: "Even in the most intricate ensemble scenes, Mozart succeeds in portraying each situation from the inside and outside simultaneously, both the subjective experience of those taking part and the objective panorama of the action as the audience experiences it." There is Mozartian magic, both attentive and inventive, in Pizzigoni's hand.

Mozart lived for scarcely two months after *The Magic Flute* was first performed. In November, he fell ill, fearing he had somehow been poisoned. For fifteen days, during his final struggle with acute rheumatic fever, his body swelled and he was wracked by spells of vomiting, until his sufferings ended on December 5. The afternoon before he died, two of the cast members of *The Magic Flute* visited him and helped him work on the Requiem—until Mozart broke down in tears, unable to go on. Later that night, he lapsed into a delirium. *The Magic Flute,* into which he had poured so much exuberant life, was his refuge in death. With almost his last words, whispered to his wife, he imagined he was back in the theater, a part of the audience at a performance of his opera. His sister-in-law, Josepha Hofer, was singing the Queen of the Night's great aria. Candles were blazing. The Queen's anger was surging. "Listen!" Mozart murmured. "Hofer is taking her top F. Now, how strongly she takes and holds the B flat. 'Hört! hört! hört! der Mutter Schwur!'" *Hear, vengeful gods, a mother's curse!* It is at once the opera's darkest and its most virtuosic moment. All of Mozart's canny and humane understanding of the motives of his characters, and of the abilities of his singers, is concentrated in this breathtakingly brilliant aria. In a sense, then, in his last moments Mozart was listening to the power of his own music, its immortal blending of passion with serene detachment, its gloriously ascendant freedom.

An impulse to freedom was the keynote to Mozart's life. Of course one hears that in the music; the very earliest compositions are marked by febrile changes of mood within the conventional forms. And nearly all his dealings with others were dominated by his urge to be free of any authority or control other than that of his own desire to write music. In *The Magic Flute,* his very last completed composition, the final freedom is love itself. Some of its characters—the Queen and Monostatos—are blinded by their passions and destroyed by their anarchic instincts. Papageno is content with mere appetite and habit. But the opera's young lovers, Tamino and Pamina, give up their freedom for love's sake, and in doing so discover a still greater freedom, encouraged by reason and goodness. They discover that love's dependence, one on another, husband on wife, lover on beloved, frees them of repressive jealousies and ungenerous feelings. In joining together, they are free to be themselves, and something more than themselves. *The Magic Flute* poignantly dramatizes their trial the better to celebrate their victory. In their happiness we are meant to find an image of what is possible for ourselves. In Mozart's music—radiant, sovereign, tender—we can hear the heart's own yearnings and struggles. We can hear the rare balance of the comic and the solemn, the melancholy and romantic and mysterious—which is, finally, the laughter in the soul.

THE STORY OF THE OPERA

ACT ONE

A handsome young prince, Tamino, is fleeing a monstrous serpent. He calls out in vain for help, then falls into a terrified faint. Three Ladies, attendants to the fabled Queen of the Night, come to his rescue and kill the serpent. While they gaze on the unconscious youth, they admire his beauty, each wanting him for herself. They withdraw, and a gaily feathered bird-catcher, Papageno, strolls in. Tamino awakens and questions him. Papageno tells him he catches birds for the Queen of the Night in exchange for food and drink, which the Three Ladies bring him each day. He then boasts of having slain the serpent in order to save the prince. The Ladies emerge and offer Papageno water instead of wine, a stone instead of sweet cake, and instead of figs a golden padlock, which they fasten to his mouth while scolding him for lying. To Tamino they give a portrait of the Queen's daughter, Pamina, the sight of which fills him with rapture. The Ladies explain that the girl has been kidnapped by an evil wizard named Sarastro.

There is a sudden burst of thunder, and the mountain parts to reveal the Queen of the Night herself. She describes her embittered sorrow at the loss of her daughter and promises Tamino the girl's hand in marriage if he can only rescue her. The mountains close over her again. The Ladies remove Papageno's padlock, once he promises never to lie again. At the Queen's bidding, they give Tamino a magic flute and Papageno a set of magic bells as protection on their journey to Sarastro's palace. They also explain that Three Spirits will lead them on their way.

In a room of Sarastro's palace, the Moorish slave Monostatos is threatening Pamina and attempts to seduce her despite her anguished pleas. Papageno happens by and peers in the window. When Monostatos and Papageno notice one another, both are frightened and they run away in opposite directions. But Papageno returns and promises Pamina that she will soon be rescued by a prince who has fallen in love with her. Meanwhile, the Three Spirits have led Tamino to a grove where stand three temples, to Wisdom, to Reason, and to Nature. Awed by the grandeur of the temples, Tamino tries to gain entrance to each but is denied, and the Old Priest he questions explains that he has been deceived by the Queen: Sarastro is not a monster but the wise leader of the sacred Brotherhood within the Temple of Wisdom. Tamino is also told that Pamina is still alive. Overjoyed, he plays upon his magic flute, and animals of all kinds approach to listen. Papageno's pipe is heard as if in response to Tamino's flute, but they cannot find each other, and Tamino rushes off in search of Pamina.

Papageno and Pamina, fleeing from the evil Monostatos and his slaves, are meanwhile searching for Tamino. When Monostatos is about to seize the pair, Papageno plays upon his magic bells, so that the slaves fall under the music's spell and dance away, allowing Papageno and Pamina to escape again. A solemn fanfare sounds, and Sarastro enters with his priests. Pamina kneels before him and asks to be forgiven for having tried to escape, explaining Monostatos's treachery and her mother's grief. Monostatos now leads in the captive Tamino. Sarastro unexpectedly punishes Monostatos and turns beneficently to the lovers to tell them they must undergo an ordeal of purification before they can be united.

ACT TWO

Sarastro tells the assembled Brotherhood that he wants Tamino to become a member of their sacred band after undergoing the necessary trials. It was for Tamino, he explains, that he separated Pamina—destined by the gods to marry the young prince—from her wicked mother. The priests signify their agreement, and Sarastro prays to the gods Isis and Osiris that the lovers be granted wisdom and strength during their ordeal.

Tamino and Papageno are told by the Two Priests of the trials awaiting them and promised that if they pledge themselves to silence each will be granted his desire—Pamina for Tamino, and Papagena for Papageno. The Three Ladies return and, predicting disaster, try to tempt the two men to break their vow. Tamino has difficulty restraining Papageno from speaking.

In a garden where she is sleeping, Monostatos again sneaks up on Pamina. This time, the Queen of the Night intervenes to save her. When Pamina tells her that Tamino has decided to join the Brotherhood, the angry Queen swears her revenge and gives her daughter a dagger, demanding that she kill Sarastro. The Queen vanishes, and Monostatos snatches the dagger from Pamina and is about to kill her when Sarastro arrives to save her.

Tamino and Papageno are led by priests into a great hall, where again they are enjoined to silence. Papagena, disguised as an old crone, enters and teasingly banters with Papageno before hobbling away. The Three Spirits appear next and present Tamino and Papageno with their magic instruments, the flute and the bells. When Tamino begins to play, Pamina at last appears. True to his vow, Tamino remains silent, puzzling his beloved. In a great vault, Sarastro bids Tamino to undergo one more grievous trial. He must bid Pamina a last farewell. The lovers part sadly.

Papageno, enjoying a glass of wine that has magically appeared, is asked by one of the priests what he most desires. A little wife, he replies. The old crone comes in and asks Papageno to marry her. With a reluctant cheerfulness, he decides a crone is better than nothing, and agrees—at which point Papagena's disguise disappears. As he rushes to embrace her, a priest keeps them apart, and Papageno sinks to the ground.

In a garden, the Three Spirits watch as Pamina, in her despair, is about to turn the dagger on herself. To stop her, they reassure her of Tamino's love. In a mountain ravine, two Men in Armor lead Tamino to the start of his trials by fire and water. Pamina is reunited with him and allowed to accompany him on the perilous path. She pledges her devotion and leads the way.

Papageno, alone again, calls and calls for his Papagena, but there is only silence all around. He decides he will hang himself to end his sorrows. The Three Spirits prevent this and urge him to play his magic bells. When he does, Papagena appears for a joyful reunion.

In her mountain fortress, the Queen plots with Monostatos and her Three Ladies to storm Sarastro's palace and have their bloody revenge. When, amid thunder and lightning, the forces of darkness attack, they are destroyed and plunged into endless night. Sunlight bursts out in glory. Sarastro and his priests, Tamino, and Pamina are seen assembled. Sarastro pronounces his blessing, and a final chorus praises the gods and the young lovers: "Brave hearts have won the glorious crown! / May Beauty to Wisdom forever be bound!"

The Magic Flute

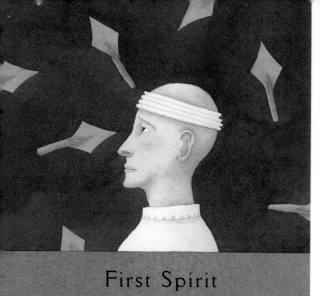

First Spirit

Sarastro

Second Lady

First Lady

Papageno

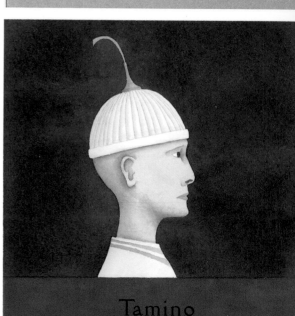

Tamino

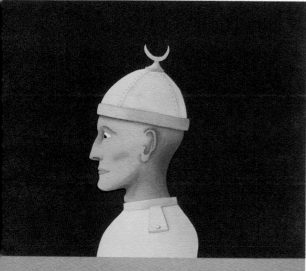

First Man in Armor

Second Spirit

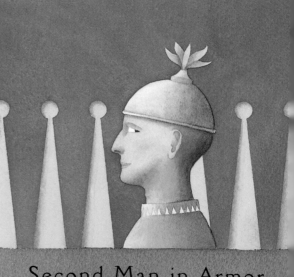

Second Man in Armor

Papagena

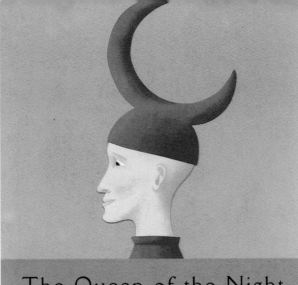

The Queen of the Night

First Priest

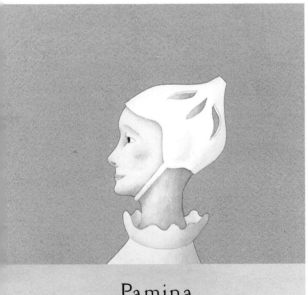

Pamina

Third Spirit

Third Lady

Second Priest

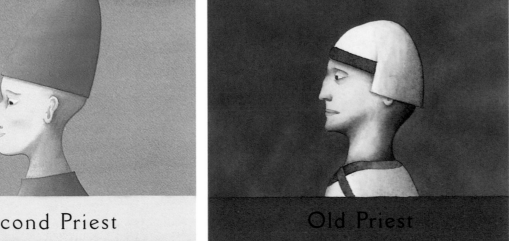

Old Priest

Monostatos

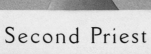

Overture

ACT ONE

FIRST SCENE

A barren, rocky
mountainside. Tamino
runs in, carrying a
bow but no arrows.
A monstrous serpent
pursues him.

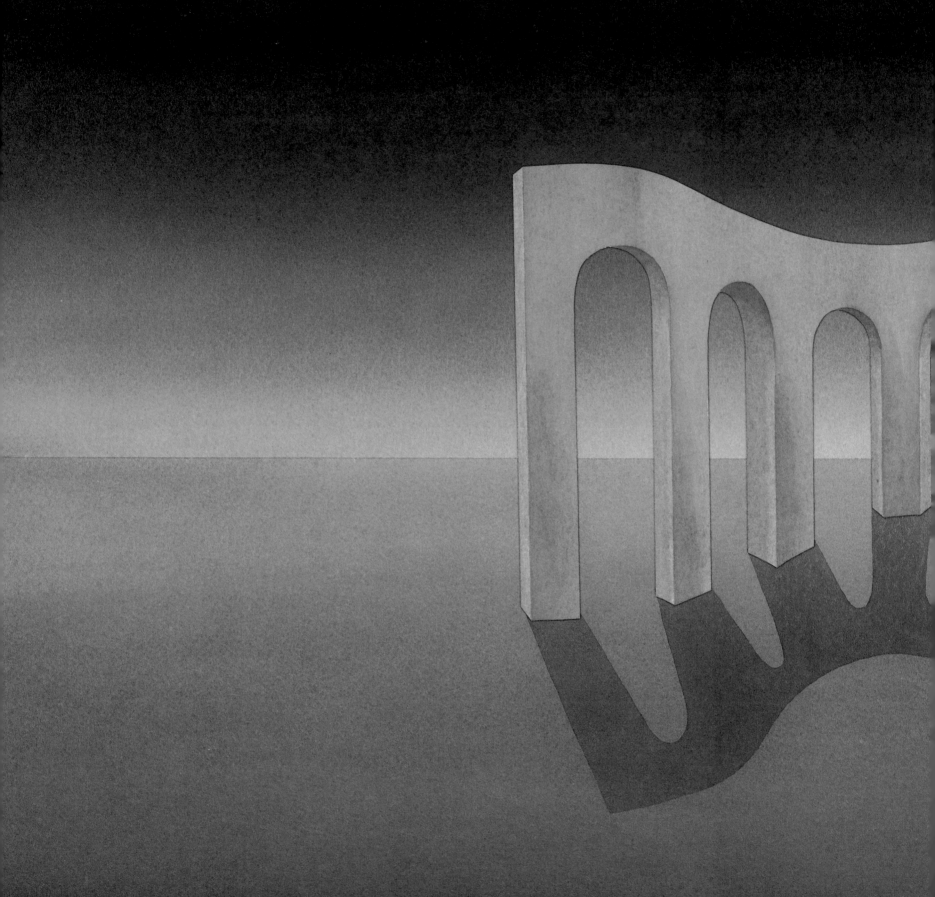

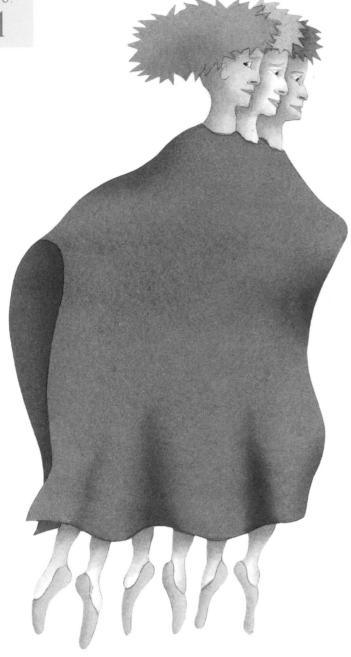

Zu Hilfe! Zu Hilfe! Sonst bin ich verloren,
Der listigen Schlange zum Opfer erkoren !
Barmherzige Götter!
Schon nahet sie sich!
Ach, rettet mich!
Ach, schützet mich!
(Er fällt in Ohnmacht. Drei verschleierte Damen
kommen herein, jede mit einem silbernen Wurfspieß.)

Help me! Help! Or else I'm lost,
Crushed between this monster's jaws!
Have mercy, gods! It's almost here!
Oh, save me from my darkest fear!
(*He faints. Three veiled Ladies enter,
each with a silver spear.*)

Die, foul monster, by our power!
(They stab the serpent.)
The final triumph now is ours!
At last your helpless victim's free,
Thanks to our swift bravery!
Stirb, Ungeheuer, durch unsre Macht!
(Sie durchbohren die Schlange.)
Triumph! Triumph! Sie ist vollbracht,
Die Heldentat. Er ist befreit
Durch unsres Armes Tapferkeit.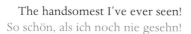

(gazing at Tamino)
A handsome youth. How sweet, how fair!
(Tamino betrachtend)
Ein holder Jüngling, sanft und schön!

The handsomest I've ever seen!
So schön, als ich noch nie gesehn!

Like a picture, lying there!
Ja, ja! Gewiß, zum Malen schön!

If ever love could sway my heart
This youth alone would have the art.
Come, let's hasten to our Queen
To tell her all that we have seen.
Perhaps this lad himself may find
Some way to give her peace of mind.
Würd' ich mein Herz der Liebe weihn,
So müßt' es dieser Jüngling sein,
Laßt uns zu unsrer Fürstin eilen,
Ihr diese Nachricht zu erteilen:
Vielleicht, daß dieser schöne Mann
Die vor'ge Ruh ihr geben kann.

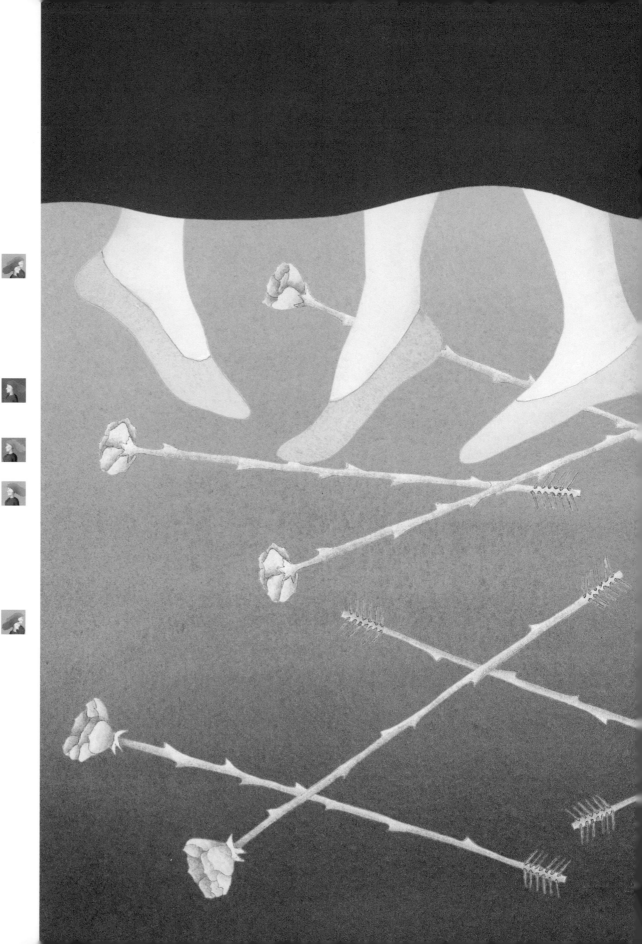

You go on. We may be late.
I'll remain with him and wait.
So geht und sagt es ihr,
Ich bleib indessen hier.

No! Your urgent task is great.
I'll watch out for him and wait.
Nein, nein! Geht ihr nur hin,
Ich wache hier für ihn!

Why this wrangling and debate?
I'll protect him while I wait.
Nein, nein! Das kann nicht sein,
Ich schütze ihn allein.

I'll remain with him and wait!
Ich bleib indessen hier!

I'll watch out for him and wait!
Ich wache hier für ihn!

I'll protect him while I wait!
Ich schütze ihn allein!

I'll remain!
Ich bleibe!

I'll watch out!
Ich wache!

I'll protect!
Ich schütze!

Ich, ich, ich!
(jede für sich)
Ich sollte fort? Ei, ei! Wie fein!
Sie wären gern bei ihm allein.
Nein, nein, das kann nicht sein!
Was wollte ich darum nicht geben,
Könnt ich mit diesem Jüngling leben!
Hätt ich ihn doch so ganz allein!
Doch keine geht, es kann nicht sein.
Am besten ist es nun, ich geh'.

 I! I! I!
(each to herself)
They stay behind? And I go home?
Each one wants him for her own!
This is no time to leave them alone!
The longer I stay, the more I yearn.
One secret glance and my heart burns.
Is there a way we two might flee?
But no one moves. It's not to be.
It's best if I myself depart.

(zusammen)
Du Jüngling, schön und liebevoll,
Du trauter Jüngling, lebe wohl,
Bis ich dich wieder seh'.
(Sie gehen alle drei ab.)

(erwacht)
Wo bin ich? Ist's Phantasie, daß ich noch lebe?
Oder hat eine höhere Macht mich gerettet?
Die Schlange tot zu meinen Füssen? Was hör' ich?
Eine seltsame Gestalt naht sich dem Tal.
(versteckt sich hinter einem Baum)

(together)
O noble youth, you have my heart!
O sweet stranger, farewell then!
Farewell! Until we meet again!
(The Ladies withdraw.)

 (waking)
Where am I? Is this a dream or do I live?
Has some higher power come to save me?
The monstrous serpent dead at my feet?
What's this? A stranger's approaching.
(hides behind a tree)

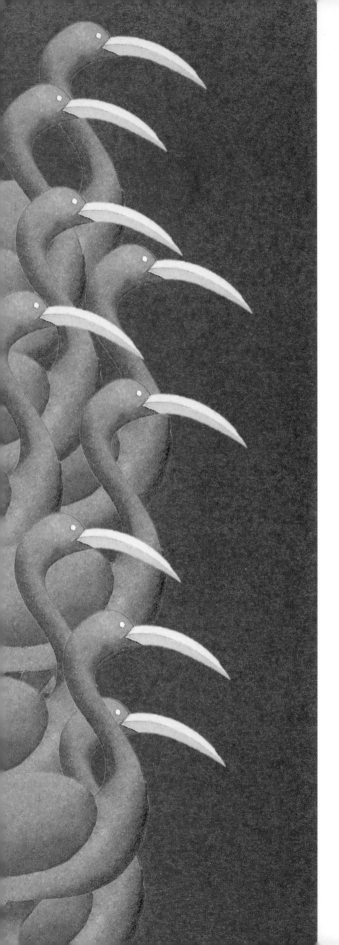

SECOND SCENE

Papageno comes down a footpath, a large birdcage on his back, a panpipe in his hand.

Der Vogelfänger bin ich ja,	A jolly trapper of birds am I
Stets lustig, heisa, hopsassa!	And tra-la-la is what I cry.
Ich Vogelfänger bin bekannt	The Bird-catcher is how I'm known,
Bei alt und jung im ganzen Land.	In every corner, by child or crone.
Weiß mit dem Locken umzugehn	My snares are laid. My sights are set.
Und mich aufs Pfeifen zu verstehen.	I just whistle them into my net.
Drum kann ich froh und lustig sein,	Mine's the life, so gay and free,
Denn alle Vögel sind ja mein.	For all the birds belong to me!

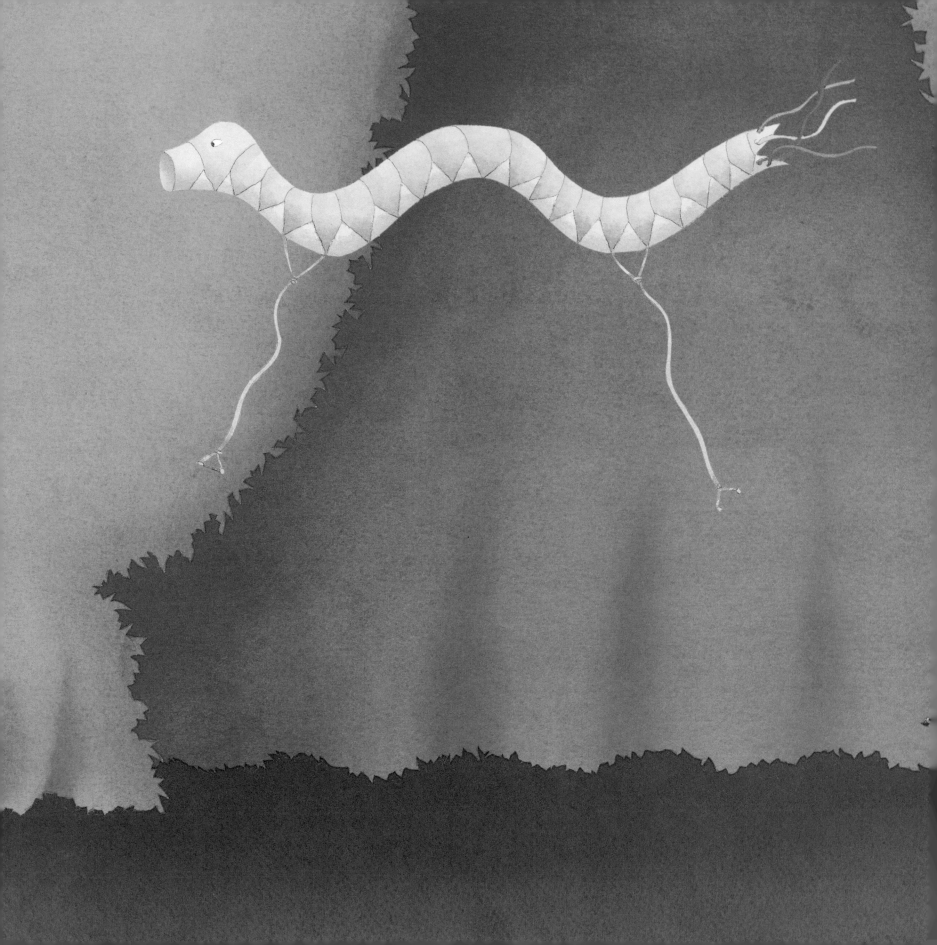

Der Vogelfänger bin ich ja,
Stets lustig, heisa, hopsassa!
Ich Vogelfänger bin bekannt
Bei alt und jung im ganzen Land.
Ein Netz für Mädchen möchte ich,
Ich fing' sie dutzendweis für mich.
Dann sperrte ich sie bei mir ein,
Und alle Mädchen wären mein.

Wenn alle Mädchen wären mein,
So tauschte ich brav Zucker ein:
Die, welche mir am liebsten wär',
Der gäb' ich gleich den Zucker her.
Und küßte sie mich zärtlich dann,
Wär' sie mein Weib und ich ihr Mann.
Sie schlief' an meiner Seite ein,
Ich wiegte wie ein Kind sie ein.

A jolly trapper of birds am I
And tra-la-la is what I cry.
The Bird-catcher is how I'm known,
In every corner, by child or crone.
If only there were traps for girls,
I'd catch a dozen by their curls.
I'd keep them in a cage, you'd see,
For all would then belong to me!

When I'd got them nice and plump,
I'd trade some for a sugar lump,
Then give it to my favorite one
And woo her till her heart was won.
And if she'd kiss me tenderly
I'd ask her next to marry me.
Then snuggled in my nest we'd lie
And rock and rock to a lullaby.

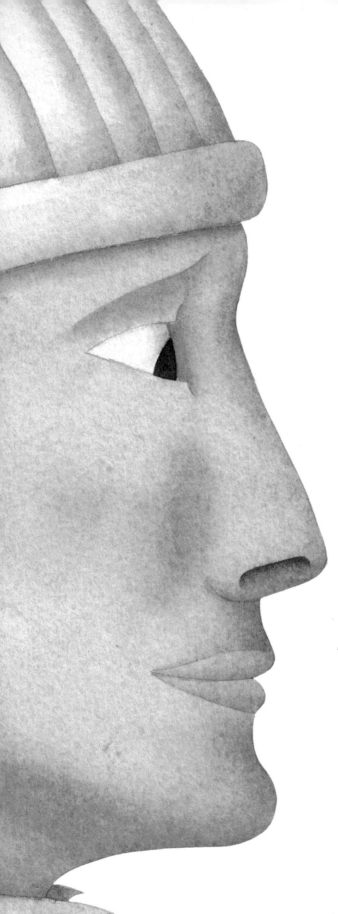

He da!

Hey there!

Sag mir, du lustiger Freund, wer du bist.

Tell me, my jolly friend, who are you?

So würde ich dir antworten, daß ich ein Prinz bin.

Since you ask, I am a prince.

Mein Vater ist ein Fürst, er herrscht
über viele Länder und Menschen.

My father is a king who rules over
many lands and peoples.

Viele Tausende!

Many thousands!

Nun sag du mir, wie nennt man eigentlich diese
Gegend? Wer beherrscht sie?

Now tell me, what is this country called,
and who is your ruler?

Aber wie lebst du?

But how do you live?

Und wie bekommst du das?

And how do you come by them?

Sternflammende Königin?

Star-shimmering Queen?

(für sich)
Wenn es gar die Königin der Nacht wäre!
(laut)
Sag mir, guter Freund, warst du schon
so glücklich, sie zu sehen?

(to himself)
Could this be the fabled Queen of the Night?
(to Papageno)
Tell me, my friend, have you been lucky
enough to see her?

Weil ich zweifle, ob du ein Mensch bist. Nach
deinen Federn, die dich bedecken, halt' ich dich . . .
(geht auf ihn zu)

Because I doubt you can be a mere mortal. By the
look of the feathers on you, I'd take you for . . .
(goes closer)

Riesenkraft?
(Er betrachtet die Schlange.)
Dann warst du wohl mein Retter, der diese
giftige Schlange bekämpfte?

The strength of a giant?
(looking down at the dead serpent)
Then are you my savior? You killed this venomous
serpent and rescued me?

Aber um alles in der Welt, Freund, wie
hast du dieses Ungeheuer besiegt?
Du bist ja ohne Waffen!

For all the world, my friend, how did you
slay this monster?
And without a weapon?

Du hast sie also erdrosselt?

You strangled it?

Who's there?	Was da!
A stupid question. I'm a man like you. Now may I ask, sir, who are you?	Wer ich bin? Dumme Frage! Ein Mensch, wie du. Und wenn ich dich nun fragte, wer du bist?
A what?	Was?
Lands? Peoples? Prince? First tell me, are there other lands and other people beyond these mountains?	Länder? Menschen? Prinz? Sag du mir zuvor: gibt's hinter diesen Bergen auch noch Länder und Menschen?
That would add some business for my trade in birds.	Da ließ' sich eine Spekulation mit meinen Vögeln machen.
If I could answer that, I could tell you too how I came into the world. All I know is that my little straw hut is nearby, and it shelters me from rain and cold.	Das kann ich dir ebensowenig beantworten, als ich weiß, wie ich auf die Welt gekommen bin. Ich weiß nur so viel, daß nicht weit von hier meine Strohhütte steht, die mich vor Regen und Kälte schützt.
By food and drink, like other men.	Von Essen und Trinken, wie alle Menschen.
By trading. I catch pretty birds for the star-shimmering Queen and her ladies . . .	Durch Tausch. Ich fange für die sternflammende Königin und ihre Damen verschiedene Vögel . . .
. . . and get in turn from them my daily food and drink.	. . . dafür erhalt' ich täglich Speis' und Trank von ihr.
See her? See the star-shimmering Queen? What mere mortal can claim to have seen her? *(to Tamino)* Why do you look at me so suspiciously?	Sehen? Die sternflammende Königin sehen? Welcher Sterbliche kann sich rühmen, sie je gesehen zu haben? *(laut)* Warum siehst du so verdächtig nach mir?
. . . for a bird? Back off! I have the strength of a giant!	Doch für keinen Vogel? – Bleib zurück, sag ich, denn ich habe Riesenkraft!
Serpent? *(looks around and retreats in fear)*	Schlange? *(sieht sich um, weicht zitternd zurück)*
Never need them. The force of my grip is stronger than any weapon	Ich brauch' keine! Bei mir ist ein starker Druck mit der Hand mehr als Waffen.
Strangled it!	Erdrosselt!

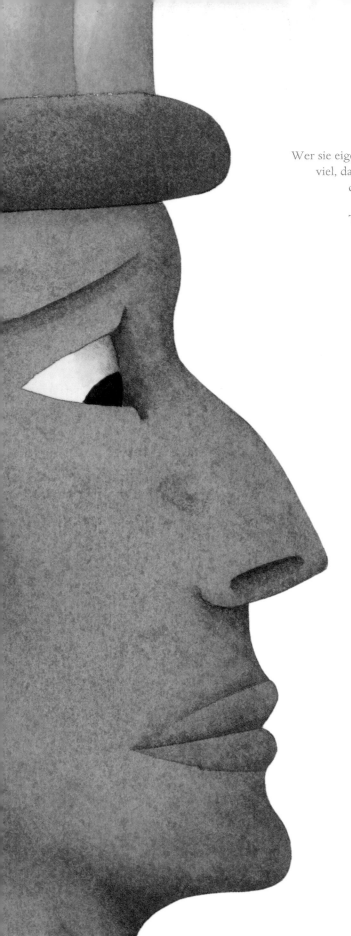

Aha, das geht mich an!	Ah, that's for me!
Wer sie eigentlich sind, weiß ich selbst nicht. Ich weiß nur so viel, daß sie mir täglich meine Vögel abnehmen und mir dafür Wein, Zuckerbrot und süße Feigen bringen.	Who exactly, I don't know myself. All I know is that every day they take my birds and bring me wine, a sugarloaf, and sweet figs in exchange.
Tja, ich denke nicht! Denn wenn sie schön wären, würden sie nicht ihre Gesichter bedecken.	Probably not. If they were beautiful, after all, they wouldn't need to cover their faces so.
Sei still! Sie drohen mir schon.	Shh! They're threatening me!
Was muß ich denn heute verbrochen haben, daß sie gar so aufgebracht gegen mich sind? Hier, meine Schönen, übergeb' ich meine Vögel.	What can I have done today to make them so angry? Here, fair ladies, I have brought you my birds.
Was? Steine soll ich fressen?	I'm meant to eat a stone?
Hm!	Hm!
Hm! . . . Hm!	Hm! . . . Hm!
Hm! Hm!	Hm! Hm!

The Three Ladies enter.

Papageno! Papageno! Papageno!	Papageno! Papageno! Papageno!
Who are these ladies?	Wer sind diese Damen?
I suppose they are very beautiful?	Sie sind vermutlich sehr schön?

(menacingly) Papageno!   *(drohend)* Papageno!

(menacingly) Papageno!   *(drohend)* Papageno!

(giving him a flask of water)
For those, Her Majesty sends you today, instead of wine, this pure, clear water.
And instead of a sugarloaf, this stone.
I hope it's to your liking.

(reicht ihm eine schöne Bouteille Wasser)
Dafür schickt dir unsere Fürstin heute statt Wein reines, helles Wasser.
Und statt Zuckerbrot, diesen Stein. Ich wünsche, daß er dir wohl bekommen möge.

And instead of sweet figs, I give you this golden padlock for your mouth.
(She fastens the padlock.)

Und statt der süßen Feigen schlage ich dir dies goldene Schloß vor den Mund.

Do you wish to know why Her Majesty punishes you so strangely today?

Willst du wissen, warum die Fürstin dich heute so wunderbar bestraft?

So you will never lie to strangers again!

Damit du künftig nie mehr Fremde belügst!

And not boast of brave deeds
that others have dared.

Und dich nie mehr der Heldentaten rühmst,
die andere vollzogen haben.

Tell us now—did you slay this serpent?

Sag! Hast du diese Schlange bekämpft?

Who did then? *(Papageno shrugs.)*

Wer denn also?

(to Tamino) It was we, young man, who set you free.

Wir waren's, Jüngling, die dich befreiten.

Fear nothing. Only joy and enchantment await you.

Zittre nicht; dich erwartet Freude und Entzücken.

Here, our great Queen sends you this, a likeness of her daughter. If you find yourself not unmoved by her features . . .

Hier, dies schickt dir die große Fürstin; es ist das Bildnis ihrer Tochter. Findest du, daß diese Züge dir nicht gleichgültig sind . . .

. . . then you are destined for happiness, honor, and glory!

. . . dann ist Glück, Ehre und Ruhm dein Los.

Farewell! Until we meet again!
(They vanish, and Papageno follows.)

Auf Wiedersehen! Auf Wiedersehen!
Auf Wiedersehen!

FOURTH SCENE

Tamino alone.

Dies Bildnis ist bezaubernd schön,
Wie noch kein Auge je gesehn!
Ich fühl' es, wie dies Götterbild
Mein Herz mit neuer Regung füllt.

This portrait's beauty I adore!
Who has seen its like before?
I feel it now, this heaven-sent art
Bewitches me and fills my heart.

I cannot name this new desire,
Burning, freezing, with one fire.
Can these be pangs of love I feel?
If so, it is to love I yield!
If only I could find her here!
If only she were somewhere near!
I would—I want—tell me,
Image, what to do?
Gently first I would caress her,
And to my ardent heart I'd press her.
Forever then would I be true.

Dies Etwas kann ich zwar nicht nennen,
Doch fühl' ich's hier wie Feuer brennen.
Soll die Empfindung Liebe sein?
Ja, ja! Die Liebe ist's allein!
O wenn ich sie nur finden könnte!
O wenn sie doch schon bei mir stände!
Ich würde—würde—warm und rein—
Was würde ich?—
Ich würde sie voll Entzücken
An diesen heißen Busen drücken,
Und ewig wäre sie dann mein.

Rüste dich mit Mut und Standhaftigkeit,
schöner Jüngling! Die Fürstin . . .

. . . hat mir aufgetragen, dir zu sagen . . .

. . . daß der Weg zu deinem künftigen Glück
nunmehr gebahnt sei.

Sie hat jedes deiner Worte gehört.
Sie hat beschlossen, . . .

. . . dich glücklich zu machen. Hat dieser Jüngling,
sprach sie, auch so viel Mut und Tapferkeit, als er
zärtlich ist, o so ist meine Tochter Pamina gerettet.

So heißt die Tochter
der Königin der Nacht.

Ein mächtiger, böser Dämon hat sie ihr entrissen.

Sarastro!

Nahe an unseren Bergen. Seine Burg ist
prachtvoll und sorgsam bewacht.

Die Königin!
(Donner)
Sie kommt!—Sie kommt!—Sie kommt!

Arm yourself with courage and steadfastness,
noble youth! The Queen . . .

. . . has commanded me to say . . .

. . . the path to your future happiness
now lies open before you.

She has heard every word you have
spoken, and decided . . .

. . . to grant your happiness. If this young man's
courage, she said, is equal to his tenderness,
then my daughter Pamina will be saved.

The name of the daughter of the
Queen of the Night.

An evil wizard has stolen her away.

Sarastro!

Close to our mountains.
His castle is a grand one and closely guarded.

The Queen!
(thunder)
She comes! She comes! She comes!

The Three Ladies and Papageno return.

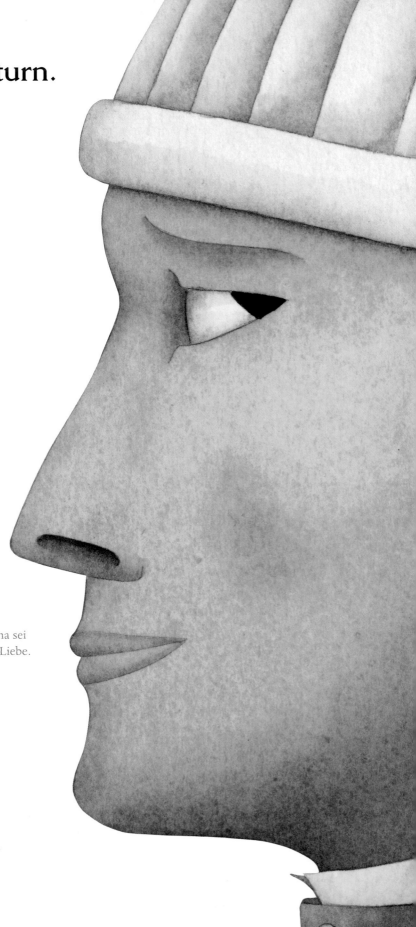

Saved? . . . Pamina?

Gerettet? . . . Pamina?

What is his name?

Wie ist sein Name?

Where does he dwell?

Wo ist sein Aufenthalt?

Come, ladies, show me the way!
Pamina will be saved! I swear it on my love.
But what's this?

Kommt, Mädchen, führt mich! Pamina sei
gerettet! Das schwör' ich bei meiner Liebe.
Ihr Götter, was ist das?

SIXTH SCENE

The mountains part
to reveal a splendid
throne room.

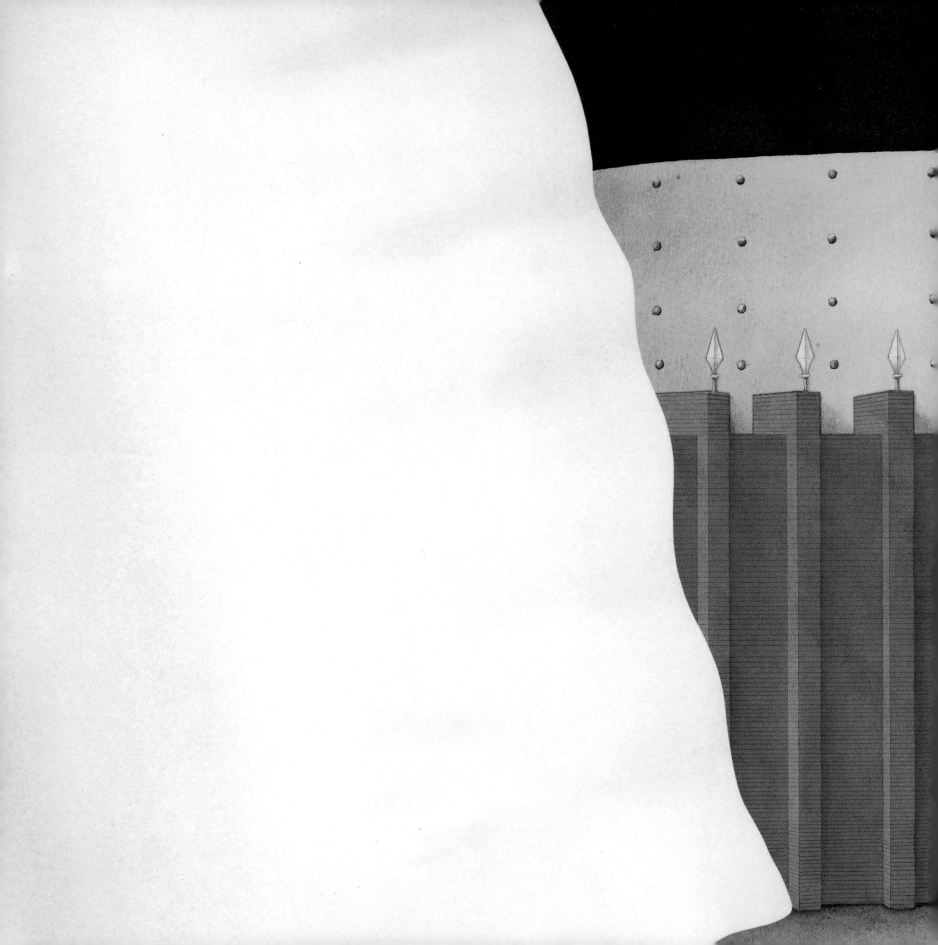

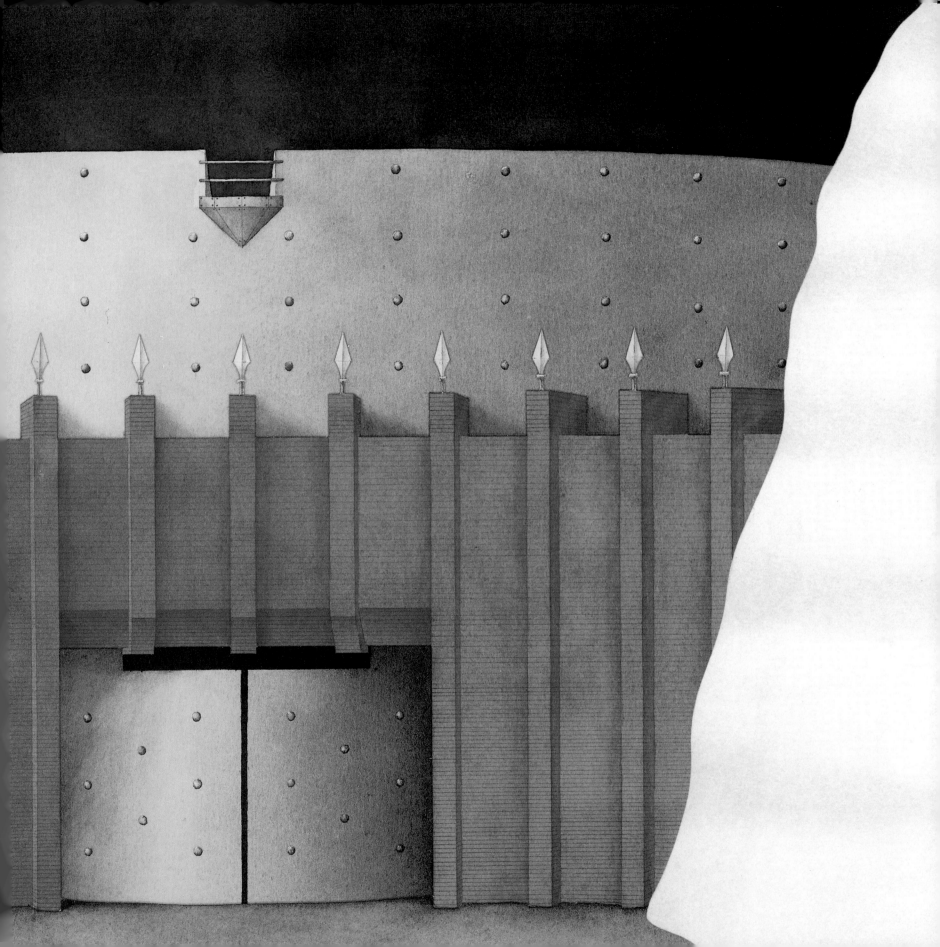

No.
4

 O zitt're nicht, mein lieber Sohn!
Du bist unschuldig, weise, fromm.
Ein Jüngling, so wie du, vermag am besten,
Dies tiefbetrübte Mutterherz zu trösten.

Zum Leiden bin ich auserkoren,
Denn meine Tochter fehlet mir;
Durch sie ging all mein Glück verloren:
Ein Bösewicht entfloh mit ihr.
Noch seh ich ihr Zittern,
Mit bangem Erschüttern
Ihr ängstliches Beben,
Ihr schüchternes Streben.
Ich mußte sie mir rauben sehen:
"Ach helft!" war alles, was sie sprach;
Allein, vergebens war ihr Flehen,
Denn meine Hilfe war zu schwach.
Du wirst sie zu befreien gehen,
Du wirst der Tochter Retter sein.
Und werd' ich dich als Sieger sehen,
So sei sie dann auf ewig dein.

Tremble not, my son, arise,
For you are innocent, pure, and wise.
Such a youth alone may heal
The wound these robes and crown conceal.

Grievous Fate's decree has stung me.
My only daughter's been stolen from me.
My happiness all vanished the day
That evil fiend stole my darling away.
I see it still before my eyes,
Her torment and her fear.
Still I hear her frightened cries
And see her anguished tears.
Helpless I watched, as if in a dream.
"Help me!" was all that she could scream.
It faded. I followed. I tore and shrieked.
But all my struggling was far too weak.
Now you shall go to set her free.
Now you can life and love restore.
And when you've won your victory
She will be yours forevermore!

SEVENTH
SCENE

Amid thunder, the
mountains close.

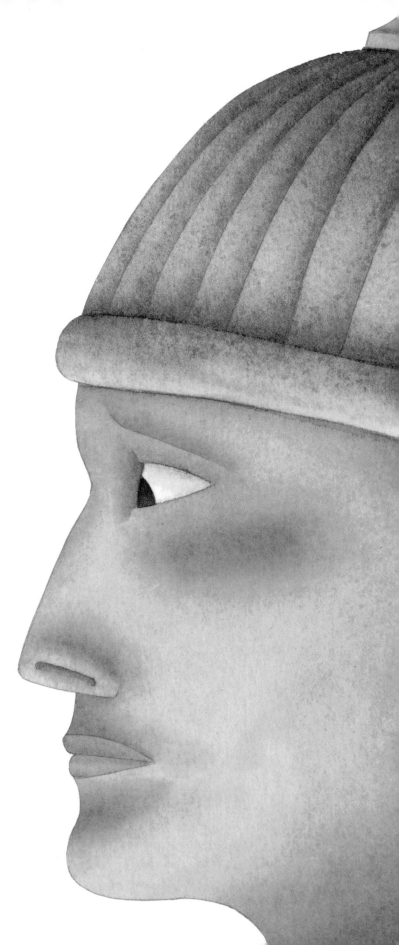

Can it be true, what I've just seen?
Gracious gods, pray don't deceive me!
Papageno!
(*Papageno approaches.*)
Ist es denn Wirklichkeit, was ich sah?
O ihr guten Götter, täuscht mich nicht!
Ha, Papageno!
(*Papageno tritt vor ihn hin.*)

· 53 ·

(pointing to the padlock on his mouth)
Hm! hm! hm! hm! hm! hm! hm! hm!
(deutet traurig auf das Schloß am Munde)
Hm, hm, hm, hm, hm, hm, hm, hm!

The poor man's punishment is plain.
His tongue is under lock and key.
Der Arme kann von Strafe sagen,
Denn seine Sprache ist dahin.

Hm! hm! hm! hm! hm! hm! hm! hm!
Hm, hm, hm, hm, hm, hm, hm, hm!

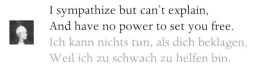

I sympathize but can't explain,
And have no power to set you free.
Ich kann nichts tun, als dich beklagen,
Weil ich zu schwach zu helfen bin.

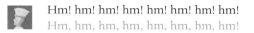

Hm! hm! hm! hm! hm! hm! hm! hm!
Hm, hm, hm, hm, hm, hm, hm, hm!

EIGHTH
SCENE

The Three Ladies

return.

(to Papageno)
The Queen has heard your mumbled plea
And bids us lift her stern decree.
(She removes the padlock.)
(zu Papageno)
Die Königin begnadigt dich,
Erläßt die Strafe dir durch mich.
(Sie nimmt ihm das Schloß vom Munde.)

At last! Again! A chatterbox!
Nun plaudert Papageno wieder!

Another lie, and double locks!
Ja, plaud're! Lüge nur nicht wieder!

I'll never tell another lie!
Ich lüge nimmermehr. Nein! Nein!

This lock should warn you not to try!
Dies Schloß soll deine Warnung sein!

This lock sure warns me not to try!
Dies Schloß soll meine Warnung sein!

All
If lies and envy could be banished
And truth alone were understood,
Then hatred, slander, all would vanish
And mankind live in brotherhood.
Bekämen doch die Lügner alle
Ein solches Schloß vor ihren Mund;
Statt Haß, Verleumdung, schwarzer Galle,
Bestünde Lieb' und Bruderbund.

(giving Tamino a flute)
Young Prince, our mighty Queen has sent
A gift to honor your consent.
This flute has strong and magic powers
To guide you through the dangerous hours.
(gibt Tamino eine goldne Flöte)
O Prinz, nimm dies Geschenk von mir!
Dies sendet unsre Fürstin dir.
Die Zauberflöte wird dich schützen,
Im größten Unglück unterstützen.

With this you can do anything.
Beasts will come and rocks will sing,
The grieving heart forget its pain
And sour hearts turn sweet again.
Hiermit kannst du allmächtig handeln,
Der Menschen Leidenschaft verwandeln:
Der Traurige wird freudig sein,
Den Hagestolz nimmt Liebe ein.

All

The spell this magic flute can cast
More than gold is worth.
It calms the soul and brings at last
Happiness on earth.
Oh, so eine Flöte ist mehr als Gold und
Kronen wert,
Denn durch sie wird Menschenglück und
Zufriedenheit vermehrt.

And now, fair ladies, there's work to do,
So may I take my leave of you?
Nun, ihr schönen Frauenzimmer,
Darf ich—so empfehl ich mich.

But listen first. You should know
The Queen's expressly chosen you.
You must stand by the Prince and go
To fight the villainous Sarastro.
Dich empfehlen kannst du immer,
Doch bestimmt die Fürstin dich,
Mit dem Prinzen ohn' Verweilen
Nach Sarastros Burg zu eilen.

That's not for me—I'm grateful, though.
You've told me he's a tiger, no?
He's sure to run me to the ground,
Then have me plucked and roasted
And feed me to his snarling hounds.
Nein, dafür bedank' ich mich!
Von euch selbsten hörte ich,
Daß er wie ein Tigertier.
Sicher ließ' ohn' alle Gnaden
Mich Sarastro rupfen, braten,
Setzte mich den Hunden für.

Dich schützt der Prinz, trau ihm allein! Dafür sollst du sein Diener sein.		Stay by the Prince and have no fear. You will be safe while he is near.
(für sich) Daß doch der Prinz beim Teufel wäre! Mein Leben ist mir lieb; Am Ende schleicht, bei meiner Ehre, Er von mir wie ein Dieb.		*(to himself)* The devil take this valiant Prince. My life means more to me. I'll bet that when the fight begins He'll be the first to flee.
(gibt Papageno ein Glockenspiel) Hier nimm dies Kleinod, es ist dein.		*(handing him a set of chimes)* This precious case is meant for you.
Ei, ei! Was mag darinnen sein?		Aha! And may I open it too?
Darinnen hörst du Glöckchen tönen.		The bells inside sound bright and true.
Werd' ich sie auch wohl spielen können?		How can I—do I strike or squeeze?
O ganz gewiß! Ja, ja, gewiß!		Oh, you can play it as you please.
Silberglöckchen, Zauberflöten Sind zu eurem Schutz vonnöten. Lebet wohl, wir wollen gehn, Lebet wohl, auf Wiedersehn!	*All*	With magic flute and silver bells A lad can cast enchanted spells. So now farewell! All's been explained. Farewell, until we meet again!
Doch, schöne Damen, saget an:		One moment, ladies. Tell me, pray—
Wie man die Burg wohl finden kann?		How are we to find our way!
Wie man die Burg wohl finden kann?		Yes, how are we to find our way?
Drei Knaben, jung, schön, hold und weise, umschweben euch auf eurer Reise; Sie werden eure Führer sein, Folgt ihrem Rate ganz allein.		Three spirit-boys are now to guide you. Along the way they'll stay beside you. If you faithfully obey, They'll be sure you never stray.
Drei Knaben, jung, schön, hold und weise, Umschweben uns auf unsrer Reise.		Three spirit-boys are now to guide us. Along the way they'll stay beside us.
So lebet wohl! Wir wollen gehn, Lebt wohl, lebt wohl! Auf Wiedersehn!	*All*	So now farewell! All's been explained. Farewell, until we meet again!

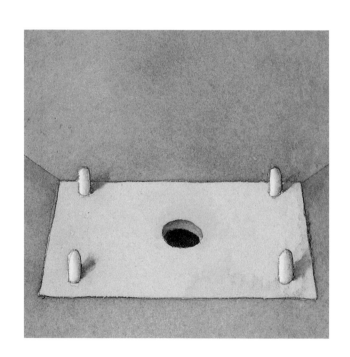

NINTH SCENE

A room in Sarastro's palace. Slaves have brought Pamina to Monostatos.

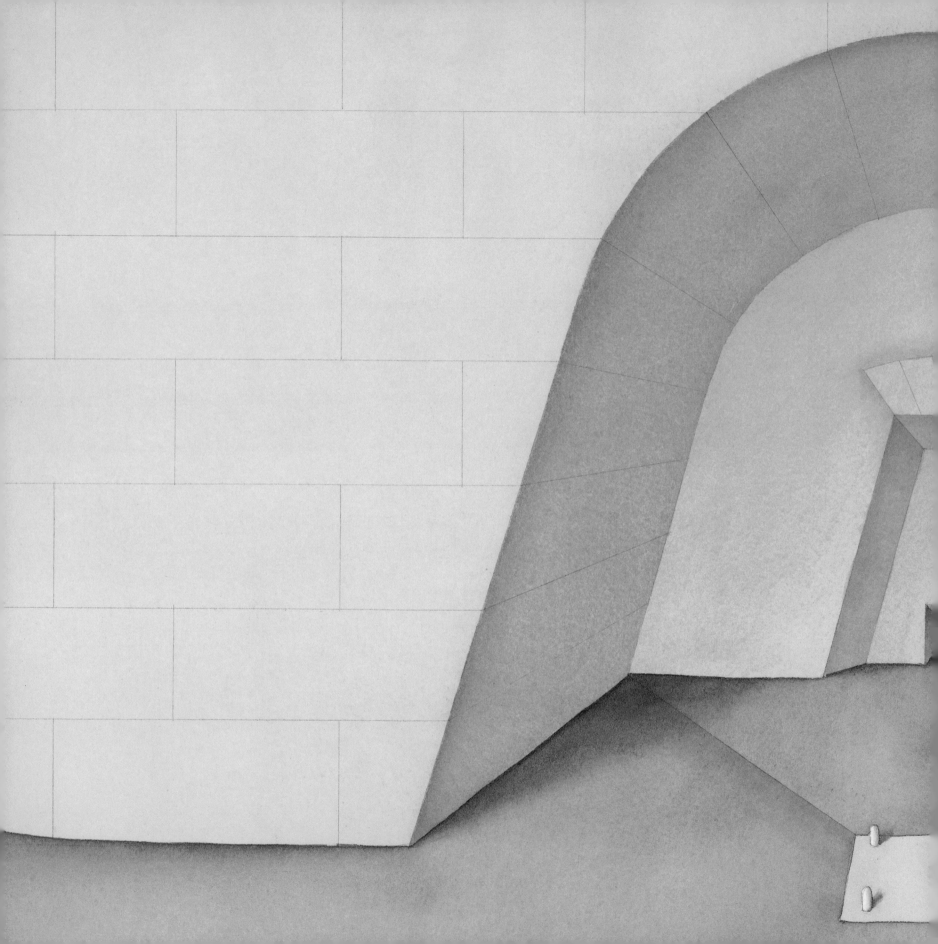

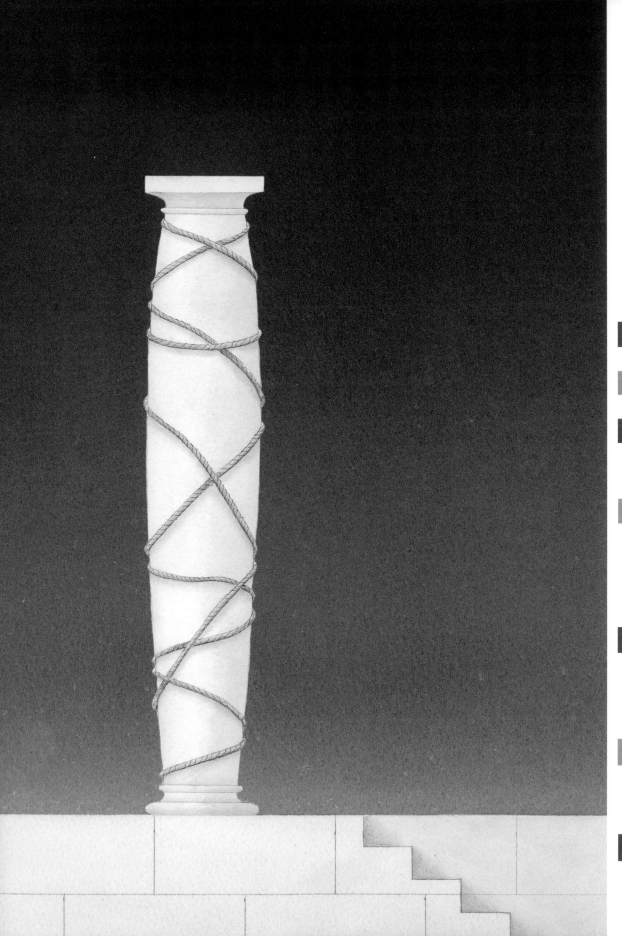

Come here, my love, you're mine again!
Du feines Täubchen nur herein!

Nothing but torment, nothing but pain!
O welche Marter! Welche Pein!

Submit or you will surely die!
Verloren ist dein Leben!

Mere death is simple to defy!
But spare me for my mother's sake.
With word of this her heart would break.
Der Tod macht mich nicht beben,
Nur meine Mutter dauert mich;
Sie stirbt vor Gram ganz sicherlich.

Slaves, bring chains!
Their effect's well known!
(They put the chains on Pamina.)
I'll force you to obey me!
He Sklaven! Legt ihr Fesseln an!
(Sie legen ihr Fesseln an.)
Mein Haß soll dich verderben.

I'd rather that you slay me!
Nothing can move a heart of stone!
(She falls onto a couch in a swoon.)
O laß mich lieber sterben,
Weil nichts, Barbar, dich rühren kann!
(Sie sinkt ohnmächtig auf ein Sofa.)

Get out! At last we are alone.
(The slaves leave hurriedly.)
Nun fort! Laßt mich bei ihr allein.
(die Sklaven gehen ab)

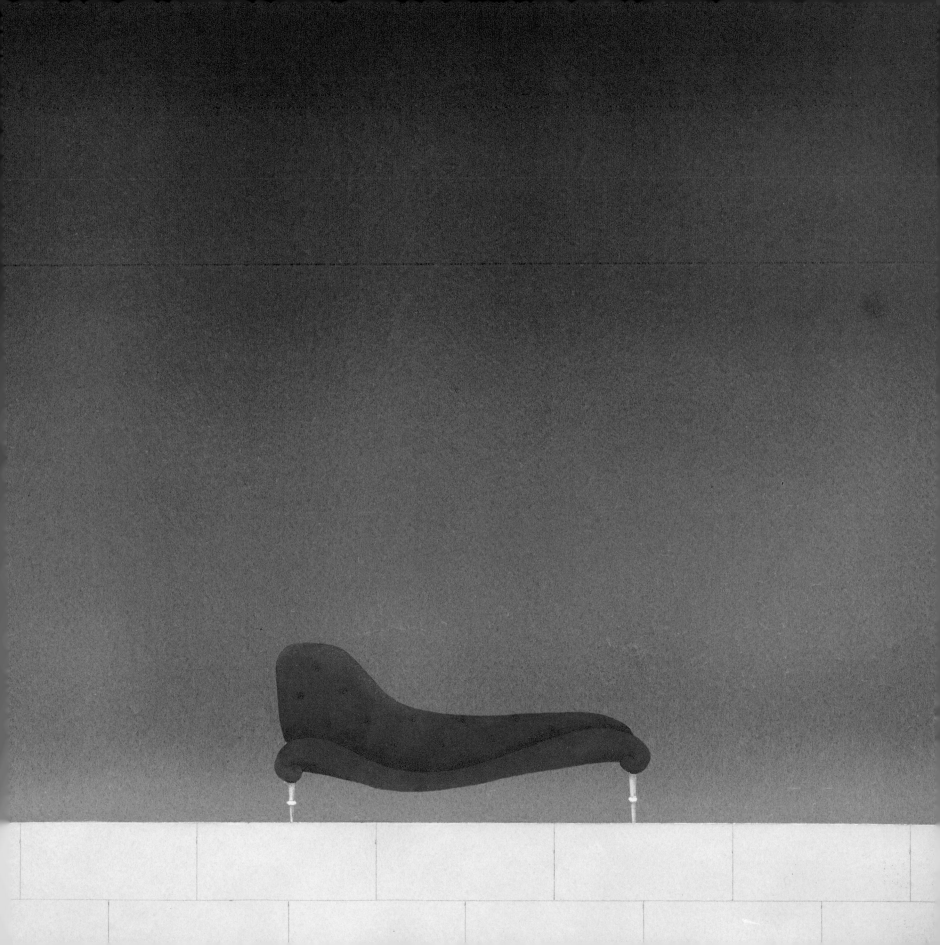

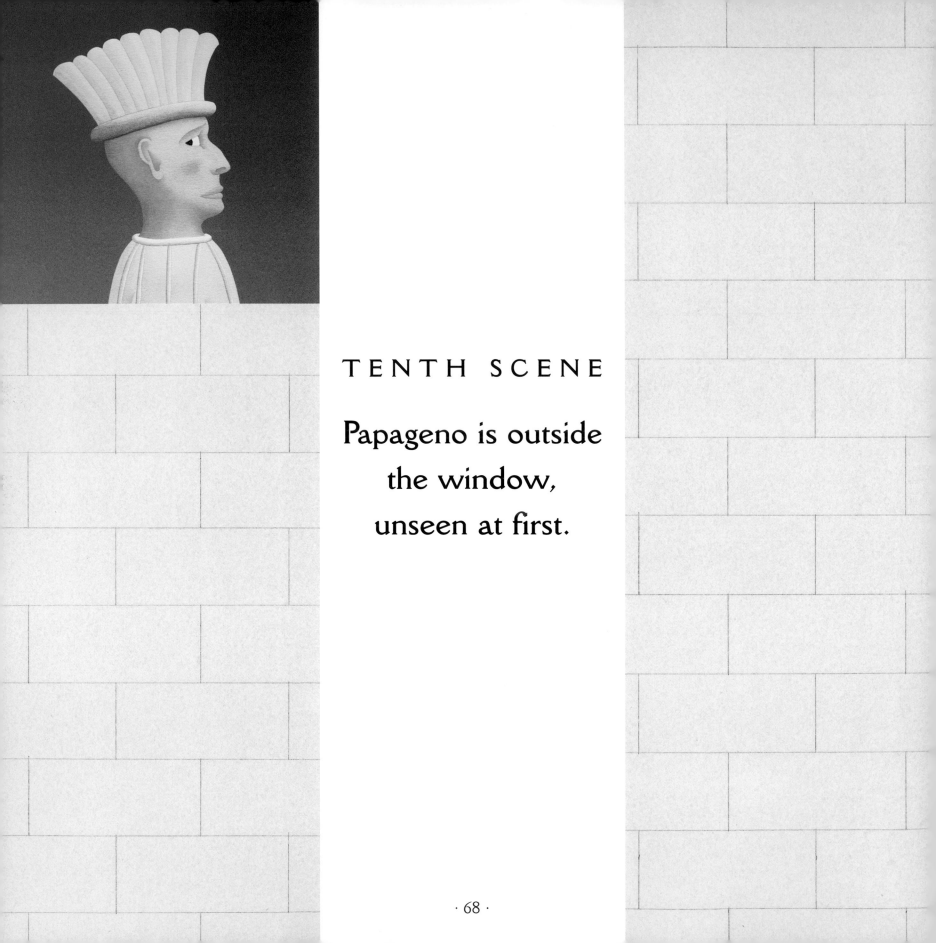

TENTH SCENE

Papageno is outside
the window,
unseen at first.

Where am I now? Where can this be?
Aha! There's someone there inside.
I'll take a chance and try to see . . .
A maiden, fair as soft moonlight,
 With skin like snow, so white!
Wo bin ich wohl? Wo mag ich sein?
Aha, da find' ich Leute!
Gewagt, ich geh' hinein.
Schön Mädchen, jung und fein,
Viel weißer noch als Kreide!

(terrified by the sight of each other)
The very devil, certainly!
Have mercy! Please! Oh, pity me!
Shoo! Shoo! Shoo!
(Monostatos runs off.)
(erschrecken einer über den andern)
Hu! das ist der Teufel sicherlich!
Hab Mitleid! Verschone mich!
Hu! hu! hu!
(Monostatos läuft davon.)

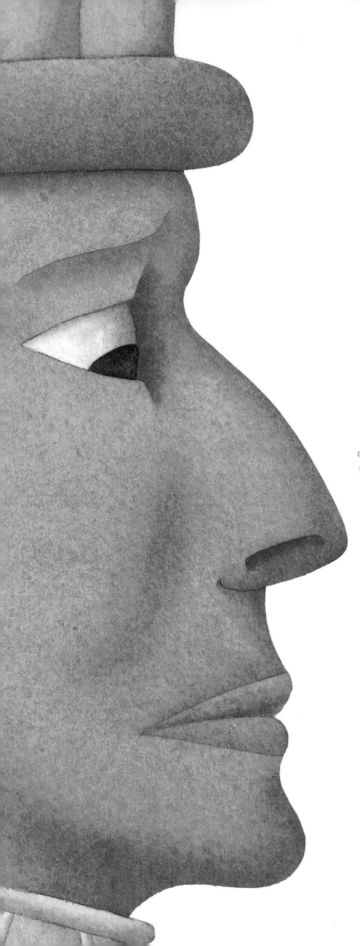

Bin ich nicht ein Narr, daß ich mich schrecken ließ? Es gibt ja schwarze Vögel in der Welt, warum denn nicht auch schwarze Menschen? Ah! Das muß Pamina sein! Du, Tochter der nächtlichen Königin . . .

What a fool I am to be so frightened! There are blackbirds in the world—so why not black men? Ah, you must be Pamina! You're the daughter of the Queen of the Night . . .

Ein Abgesandter der sternflammenden Königin.

An emissary from the star-shimmering Queen.

Papageno.

Papageno.

Ich dich auch nicht! Ich liefere deiner Mutter schon seit vielen Jahren all die schönen Vögel in den Palast.—Heute, als ich im Begriff war, meine Vögel abzugeben, sah ich plötzlich einen Menschen vor mir, der sich Prinz nennen läßt. Dieser Prinz hat deine Mutter so für sich eingenommen, daß sie ihm dein Bildnis schenkte und ihm befahl, dich zu befreien. Sein Entschluß war ebenso rasch wie seine Liebe zu dir.

Nor I you. For years I've caught all sorts of pretty birds and taken them to the palace for your mother. Today I was making my delivery when suddenly someone was standing before me who called himself a prince. Your mother was so taken with him that she gave him a portrait of you and commanded him to rescue you. He obeyed at once because he had fallen in love with you.

Der Prinz hat mich vorausgeschickt, um dir seine Ankunft anzukündigen.

The Prince has sent me on ahead to announce his arrival.

Noch nicht einmal ein Mädchen, viel weniger ein Weib! Ich möchte mir oft alle meine Federn ausrupfen, wenn ich bedenke, daß Papageno noch keine Papagena hat.

Not even a sweetheart, much less a wife! I'd as soon pull out all my feathers, when I think that Papageno has no Papagena!

Wenn er sie nur bald schickte!

If only she'd come soon!

Pamina and Papageno alone.

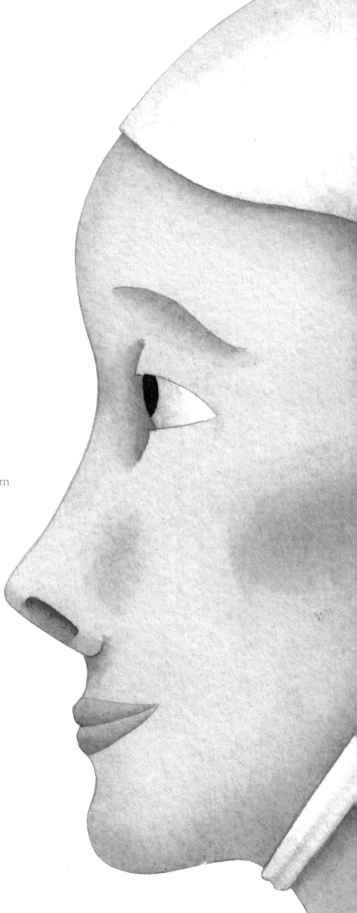

Who are you?

Wer bist du?

(joyfully)
My mother! And your name?

(freudig)
Meiner Mutter? Dein Name?

Papageno? Papageno . . . I have often heard that name before, but you yourself I've never seen.

Papageno?—Papageno . . . Den Namen hab' ich schon oft gehört! Aber ich sah dich nie!

He loves me?
Well, if it's really love he feels, why does he wait so long to rescue me?

Er liebt mich?
Ja, aber wenn er Liebe für mich empfindet, warum säumt er dann so lange, mich zu befreien?

You're very daring!
And have you a wife who is waiting for you at home?

Du hast viel gewagt!
Hast du denn noch kein Weib,
das auf dich wartet?

Patience, friend! Heaven will send her sooner than you think.

Geduld, Freund! Der Himmel wird auch dir eine Freundin schicken, eh' du's vermutest.

A man who's touched by love's emotion
Surely has a tender heart.
Bei Männern, welche Liebe fühlen
Fehlt auch ein gutes Herze nicht.

To share a man's sincere devotion—
That should be the woman's part.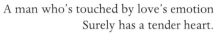
Die süßen Triebe mitzufühlen
Ist dann der Weiber erste Pflicht.

The greatest joy that each may own—
To live by love, by love alone.
Wir wollen uns der Liebe freun,
Wir leben durch die Lieb' allein.

Love can lighten every sorrow.
Every creature pays her due.
Die Lieb' versüßet jede Plage,
Ihr opfert jede Kreatur.

 Love today and love tomorrow
Keep Nature's circle turning true.
Sie würzet unsre Lebenstage,
Sie wirkt im Kreise der Natur.

The noblest aim of human life
Is to be joined as man and wife.
Man and wife, and wife and man,
Both are parts of heaven's plan.
(They both go off.)
 Ihr hoher Zweck zeigt deutlich an,
Nichts Edlers sei, als Weib und Mann.
Mann und Weib, und Weib und Mann,
Reichen an die Gottheit an.
(beide ab)

TWELFTH SCENE

A grove with three temples.
On either side are the Temple
of Reason and the Temple
of Nature. In the center is
the Temple of Wisdom. The
Three Spirits lead in Tamino.

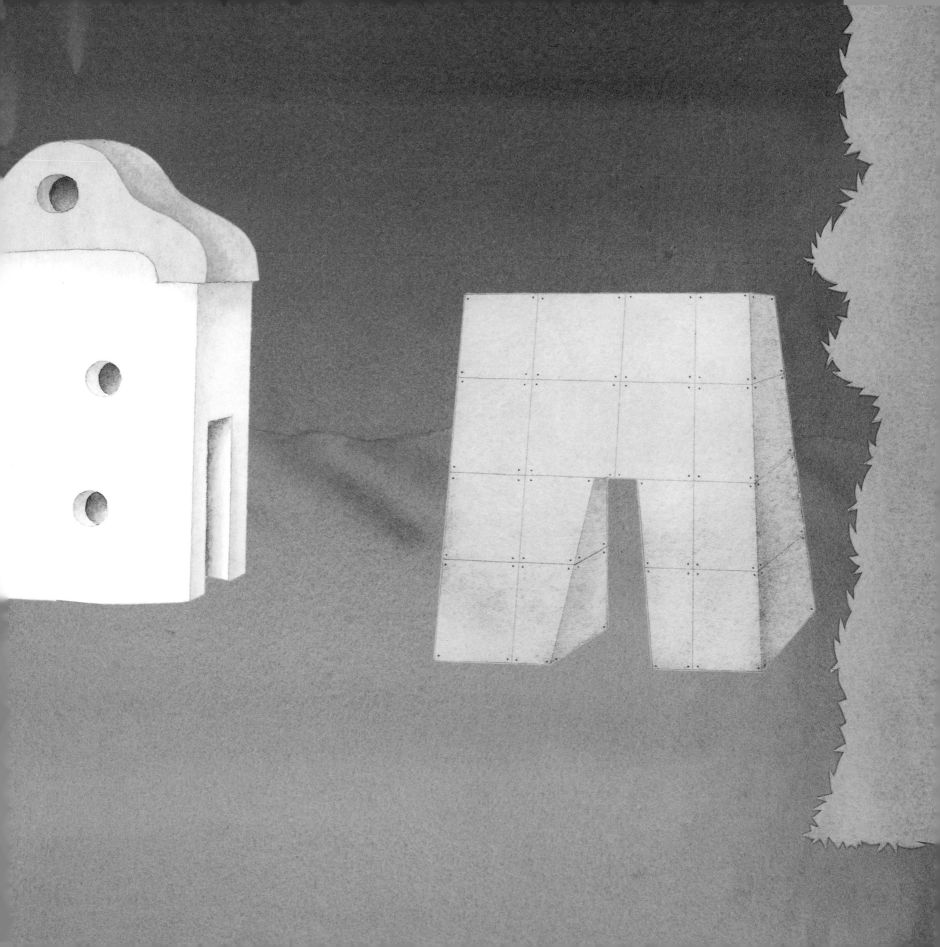

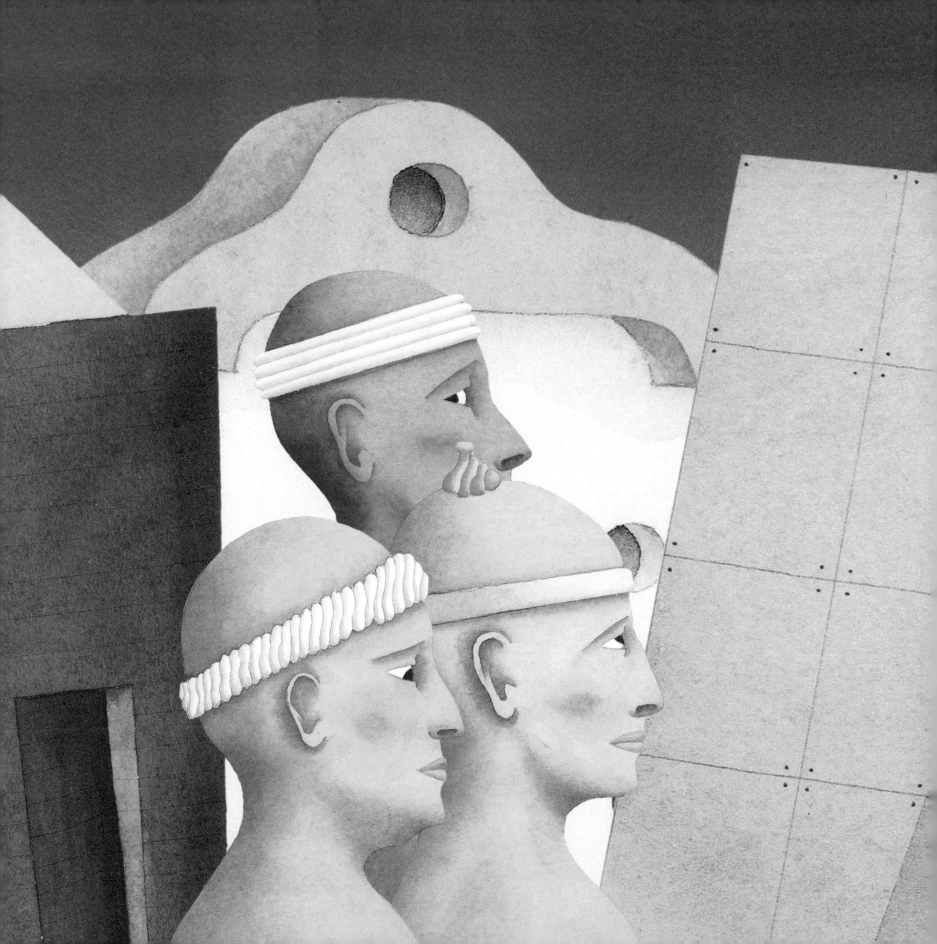

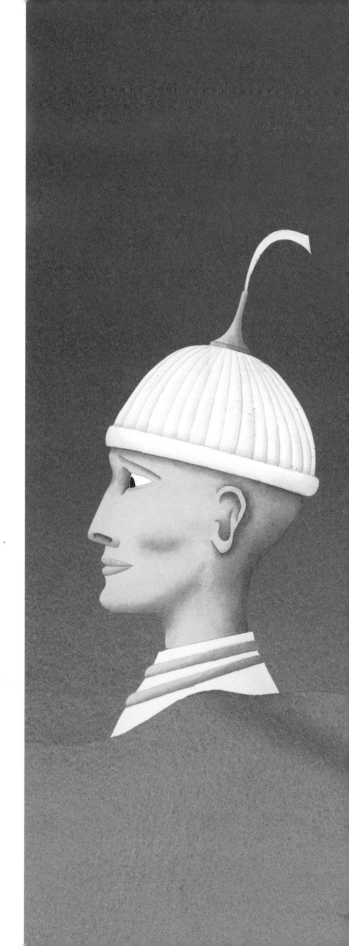

Zum Ziele führt dich diese Bahn,
Doch mußt du, Jüngling, männlich siegen.
Drum höre unsre Lehre an:
Sei standhaft, duldsam und verschwiegen!

This path will lead you on your way.
A manly spirit will not stray.
To these three virtues now hold fast—
Be silent, patient, and steadfast!

Ihr holden Knaben, sagt mir an,
Ob ich Pamina retten kann?

But, blessed spirits, first tell me—
May I set Pamina free?

Dies kund zu tun, steht uns nicht an:
Sei standhaft, duldsam und verschwiegen!
Bedenke dies; kurz, sei ein Mann,
Dann, Jüngling, wirst du männlich siegen.
(gehen ab)

The answer is not ours to tell.
Be silent, patient, and steadfast!
A manly courage most excels.
Who bravely dares will win at last!
(They leave.)

Die Weisheitslehre dieser Knaben
Sei ewig mir ins Herz gegraben.
Wo bin ich nun? Was wird mit mir?
Ist dies der Sitz der Götter hier?
Es zeigen die Pforten, es zeigen die Säulen,
Daß Klugheit und Arbeit und Künste hier weilen;
Wo Tätigkeit thronet und Müßiggang weicht,
Erhält seine Herrschaft das Laster nicht leicht.
Ich wage mich mutig zur Pforte hinein,
Die Absicht ist edel und lauter und rein.
Erzitt're, feiger Bösewicht!
Pamina retten ist mir Pflicht.
*(Er geht an die Pforte zur rechten Seite.
Man hört eine Stimme.)*

May the truths these boys impart
Be carved forever on my heart!
Where am I now! And what's inside?
Can this be where the gods abide?
It's here, these portals seem to tell,
That Skill and Work and Wisdom dwell.
Where all men strive and vigor's crowned,
No vice or baseness will be found.
All danger mocked, and death defied,
My purpose noble, my courage high,
Evil wizard, beware my scorn!
To save Pamina I have sworn!
*(As he rushes toward the temple on the right,
a voice is heard.)*

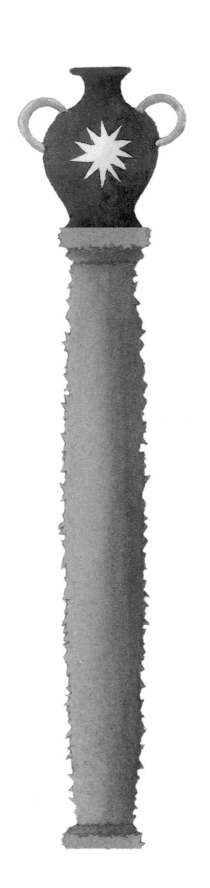

Go back!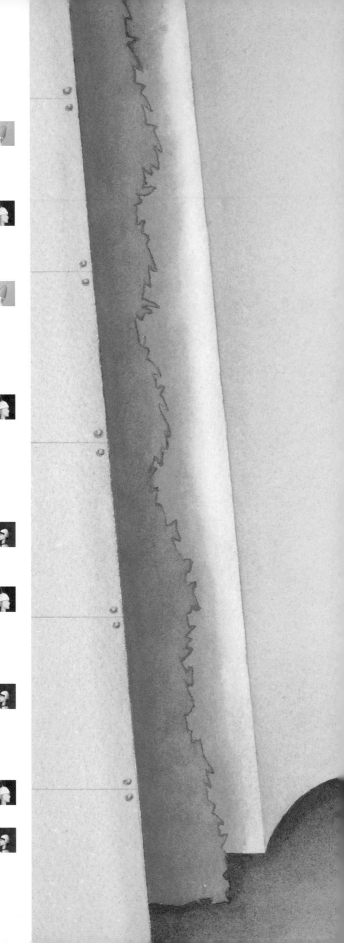
Zurück!

Go back? I'll try my fortune here!
*(He goes to the temple on the left, and again
a voice is heard.)*
Zurück? So wag' ich hier mein Glück!
*(Er geht zur linken Pforte; eine Stimme
von innen.)*

Go back!
Zurück!

"Go back, go back!" is all I hear.
(He goes to the temple in the center.)
One last door remains. I'll dare
Once more to find an entrance there.
(He knocks. An Old Priest appears.)
Auch hier ruft man: zurück!
(Er geht zur mittleren Pforte.)
Da seh' ich noch eine Tür,
Vielleicht find' ich den Eingang hier.
(Er klopft. Ein alter Priester erscheint.)

Who is it comes? Bold stranger, speak!
Why have you sought this sacred place?
Wo willst du, kühner Fremdling, hin?
Was suchst du hier im Heiligtum?

Love and Virtue are what I seek.
Der Lieb' und Tugend Eigentum.

Your words disclose a noble mind,
But success is honor's counterpart.
Love and Virtue you will never find
While death and vengeance rule your heart.
Die Worte sind von hohem Sinn!
Allein, wie willst du diese finden?
Dich leitet Lieb' und Tugend nicht,
Weil Tod und Rache dich entzünden.

Upon a fiend, revenge in kind!
Nur Rache für den Bösewicht!

Within this Temple, all's benign.
Den wirst du wohl bei uns nicht finden.

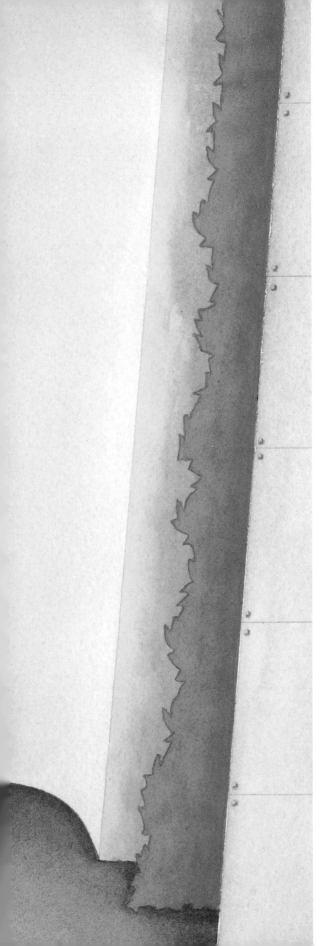

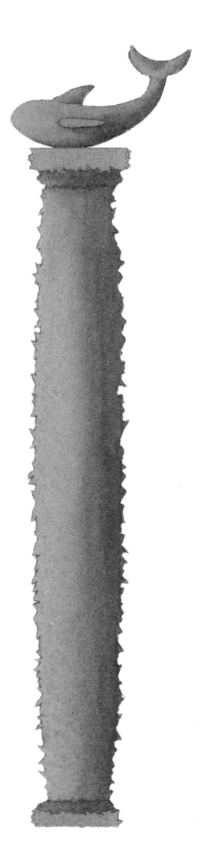

It's here the great Sarastro rules?
Sarastro herrscht in diesen Gründen?

Indeed, it's here Sarastro rules.
Ja, ja, Sarastro herrschet hier!

But not in Wisdom's sacred shrine?
Doch in dem Weisheitstempel nicht?

He rules in Wisdom's sacred shrine!
Er herrscht im Weisheitstempel hier.

So everything's hypocrisy!
So ist denn alles Heuchelei!

You wish, I gather, now to go?
Willst du schon wieder gehn?

Yes, I'll go, relieved and free—
The wisdom here is just a show.
Ja, ich will gehn, froh und frei,
Nie euren Tempel sehn!

Explain yourself to me.
I fear you've been misled.
Erklär dich näher mir,
Dich täuschet ein Betrug.

If Sarastro is your head,
That's quite enough for me.
Sarastro wohnet hier,
Das ist mir schon genug.

Listen, boy, as your life is dear.
I command you not to move from here!
It is Sarastro you hate so?
Wenn du dein Leben liebst,
So rede, bleibe da!
Sarastro hassest du?

I hate him, and the reason's clear.
Ich hass' ihn ewig! Ja!

Nun gib mir deine Gründe an.		And can you tell me how you know?
Er ist ein Unmensch, ein Tyrann!		He is a tyrant, a monstrous foe!
Ist das, was du gesagt, erwiesen?		And can you prove what you now say?
Durch ein unglücklich Weib bewiesen, Das Gram und Jammer niederdrückt.		A woman can, who day by day Suffers grief and endless woe.
Ein Weib hat also dich berückt! Ein Weib tut wenig, plaudert viel. Du, Jüngling, glaubst dem Zungenspiel? O, legte doch Sarastro dir Die Absicht seiner Handlung für!		A woman told you this was so? Foolish youth, to so believe The webs that chattering women weave. Would Sarastro himself were here At last to make his motives clear!
Die Absicht ist nur allzu klar! Riß nicht der Räuber ohn' Erbarmen Pamina aus der Mutter Armen?		His motives from the first I knew! Did not that villain connive and tear A daughter from her mother's care?
Ja, Jüngling! Was du sagst, ist wahr.		Young stranger, what you say is true.
Wo ist sie, die er uns geraubt? Man opferte vielleicht sie schon?		Where is she now? What is her plight? Has she survived this cruel ordeal?
Dir dies zu sagen, teurer Sohn, Ist jetzt und mir noch nicht erlaubt.		The secrets of the Temple's rites I am forbidden to reveal.
Erklär dies Rätsel, täusch mich nicht.		Explain your riddle! Tell me now!
Die Zunge bindet Eid und Pflicht.		I am bound to silence by my vow.
Wann also wird das Dunkel schwinden?		When are light and truth allowed?
Sobald dich führt der Freundschaft Hand Ins Heiligtum zum ew'gen Band. *(geht ab)*		When you are led by friendship's hand To join this Temple's sacred band. *(He withdraws.)*

(allein) O ew'ge Nacht! Wann wirst du schwinden?		*(to himself)* O starless night! O endless sorrow!
Wann wird das Licht mein Auge finden?		Will the answers come tomorrow?
(von innen) Bald, bald, Jüngling, oder nie!	*Chorus*	*(from within)* Soon, fair youth, or nevermore.
Bald, sagt ihr, oder nie?		Soon, they say, or nevermore?
Ihr Unsichtbaren, saget mir,		Unseen powers, answer me—
Lebt denn Pamina noch?		Is Pamina still alive?
Pamina lebet noch!	*Chorus*	Yes, Pamina's still alive!
Sie lebt! Ich danke euch dafür.		Alive! For that one word my thanks!
(Er nimmt seine Flöte heraus.)		*(He takes up his flute.)*
O, wenn ich doch imstande wäre,		If only I could find the phrases,
Allmächtige, zu eurer Ehre,		Mighty forces, to sing your praises.
Mit jedem Tone meinen Dank zu schildern,		This song comes from a heart in love.
wie er hier, hier entsprang!		Let it be heard in heaven above!
(Er spielt; sogleich kommen Tiere von allen Arten hervor, ihm zuzuhören. Er hört auf, und sie fliehen.)		*(He plays. The beasts of the forest come out to hear him. When he stops, they flee. Birds sing to his playing.)*
Wie stark ist nicht dein Zauberton,		How this magic flute enchants!
Weil, holde Flöte, durch dein Spielen		In its music spells hold sway.
Selbst wilde Tiere Freude fühlen.		The birds will sing, the beasts will dance.
Doch nur Pamina bleibt davon.		But only Pamina stays away!
Pamina! Höre, höre mich! Umsonst!		Pamina! Can you hear me call?
Wo? Ach, wo find' ich dich?		How will I ever find you at all?
(antwortet von innen mit seinem Flötchen)		*(answers on his panpipe from afar)*
Ha, das ist Papagenos Ton! *(Er spielt.)*		That is Papageno's sound! *(He plays.)*
(antwortet)		*(answers)*
Vielleicht sah er Pamina schon,		Perhaps it means Pamina's found.
Vielleicht eilt sie mit ihm zu mir!		Perhaps Pamina's by his side!
Vielleicht führt mich der Ton zu ihr.		This magic flute must be my guide!
(Er eilt ab.)		*(He runs off.)*

THIRTEENTH SCENE

Pamina and Papageno wander in.

Schnelle Füße, rascher Mut		Swift of foot and bold of heart
Schützt vor Feindes List und Wut.		Can still outrun, and still outsmart.
Fänden wir Tamino doch,		Unless we find Tamino, though,
Sonst erwischen sie uns noch!		We can't just scramble to and fro.
Holder Jüngling!		Ta-mi-no!
Stille, stille, ich kann's besser!		Shh! I know a better way!
(Er pfeift.)		*(He plays.)*
(antwortet von innen auf seiner Flöte)		*(on his flute from within)*
Welche Freude ist wohl größer?		It's closer! Yes, it does not fade!
Freund Tamino hört uns schon.		At last Tamino hears our cry.
Hierher kam der Flötenton.		His magic flute's his sweet reply.
Welch ein Glück, wenn ich ihn finde!		We'll tell all we've seen and done!
Nur geschwinde! Nur geschwinde!		Hurry now! Run! Let's run!
(Sie wollen gehen.)		*(They are about to leave.)*

FOURTEENTH SCENE

Monostatos and his slaves suddenly enter.

(ihrer spottend)		*(mocking them)*
Nur geschwinde! Nur geschwinde!		"Hurry now! Run! Let's run!"
Ha, hab ich euch noch erwischt?		Ha! Now I have you both again!
Nur herbei mit Stahl und Eisen;		Bring the heavy iron chains!
Wart, ich will euch Mores weisen.		They will teach you to obey.

Den Monostatos berücken! You both were foolish to betray!
Nur herbei mit Band und Stricken! Monostatos has won the day!
He, ihr Sklaven, kommt herbei! Bring the chains to bind them with!

Ach, nun ist's mit uns vorbei! Now all, I fear, is over with!

He, ihr Sklaven, kommt herbei! Bring the chains to bind them with!
(Sklaven kommen mit Fesseln.) (Slaves come with rope and chain.)

Wer viel wagt, gewinnt oft viel! He who dares has all to win!
Komm, du schönes Glockenspiel, Come, my chimes, let bells begin!
Laß die Glöckchen klingen, klingen, Let the precious silver ring!
Daß die Ohren ihnen singen. Let the bells sound out and sing!
(Papageno spielt auf seinem Glockenspiel. (He plays on the bells. At once
Sogleich tanzen und singen Monostatos and his slaves
Monostatos und die Sklaven.) begin to dance and sing.)

Das klinget so herrlich, It sounds so happy,
Das klinget so schön! Sounds so gay!
Larala la la larala! Larala la la larala!
Nie hab' ich so etwas gehört und gesehn! Let's sing and dance our time away!
Larala la la larala! Larala la la larala!
(Sie tanzen ab.) (They dance out.)

Könnte jeder brave Mann If every man had magic bells,
Solche Glöckchen finden, And played them to deceive,
Seine Feinde würden dann Charmed at once by music's spells,
Ohne Mühe schwinden, His enemies would leave.
Und er lebte ohne sie Music gladdens every soul
In der besten Harmonie! In perfect harmony!
Nur der Freundschaft Harmonie Life on earth's again made whole
Mildert die Beschwerden; By friendship's sympathy.
Ohne diese Sympathie Sorrows first will yield to laughter,
Ist kein Glück auf Erden! Then joy forever follows after!

Es lebe Sarastro, Sarastro lebe! *Voices* Long live Sarastro! Sarastro all hail!

Was soll das bedeuten? What's that noise those men are making?
Ich zitt're, ich bebe. And why are my feathery knees so shaking?

O Freund, nun ist's um uns getan, My friend, the day is lost, I fear.
Dies kündigt den Sarastro an. Those shouts must mean Sarastro's near!

O, wär' ich eine Maus, 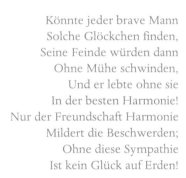 Oh, I wish I were a mouse
Wie wollt' ich mich verstecken! And so could quickly hide!
Wär' ich so klein wie Schnecken, Or had a snail's shell-house
So kröch' ich in mein Haus! To slip at once inside!
Mein Kind, was werden wir nun sprechen? What now are we supposed to say?

Die Wahrheit, sei sie auch Verbrechen! The truth! The truth! Let come what may.

FIFTEENTH SCENE

<table>
<tr><td></td><td>Es lebe Sarastro, Sarastro soll leben!
Er ist es, dem wir uns mit Freuden ergeben!
Stets mög' er des Lebens als Weiser sich freun.
Er ist unser Abgott, dem alle sich weihn.</td><td>*Chorus*</td><td>Long live Sarastro! Sarastro all hail!
Long may his tolerant vision prevail!
Long may he guide us to wisdom and light!
Sarastro's our leader, ordaining the right!</td></tr>
<tr><td></td><td>*(kniet)*
Herr, ich bin zwar Verbrecherin,
Ich wollte deiner Macht entfliehn.
Allein die Schuld liegt nicht an mir:
Der böse Mohr verlangte Liebe;
Darum, o Herr, entfloh ich dir.</td><td></td><td>*(kneeling)*
My lord, I here confess my crime.
I broke your law and tried to flee.
Yet in the end the guilt's not mine.
That wicked Moor demanded love.
What choice, my lord, was left to me?</td></tr>
<tr><td></td><td>Steh auf, erheit're dich, o Liebe!
Denn ohne erst in dich zu dringen,
Weiß ich von deinem Herzen mehr:
Du liebest einen andern sehr.
Zur Liebe will ich dich nicht zwingen,
Doch geb' ich dir die Freiheit nicht.</td><td></td><td>Arise, my child, and dry that tear.
Your story's meaning is quite clear.
And with no question on my part,
I discern the secrets of your heart.
Your true love's name is known to me,
But still I may not set you free.</td></tr>
</table>

Mich rufet ja die Kindespflicht,
Denn meine Mutter . . .

 It's not just for myself I plead.
My mother is . . .

. . . steht in meiner Macht.
Du würdest um den Glück gebracht,
Wenn ich dich ihren Händen ließe.

. . . under my control.
All's lost—the happiness foretold—
If I return you to your mother.

Mir klingt der Muttername süße!
Sie ist es . . .

Her love is truer than all others.
My mother is . . .

. . . und ein stolzes Weib!
Ein Mann muß eure Herzen leiten,
Denn ohne ihn pflegt jedes Weib
Aus ihrem Wirkungskreis zu schreiten.

. . . too swollen with pride.
A man must show your heart its way.
Without a man to stand beside,
A woman's bearings go astray.

A procession of
priests enters with
Sarastro.
Monostatos and his
slaves follow.

SIXTEENTH
SCENE

Monostatos leads
in Tamino.

Nun, stolzer Jüngling, nur hierher, Hier ist Sarastro, unser Herr.		Now, proud princeling, if you please . . . The great Sarastro! On your knees!
Er ist's!		It's he!
Sie ist's!		It's she!
Ich glaub' es kaum!		Are things what they seem?
Es ist kein Traum!		Surely this is no dream!
Es schling' mein Arm sich um ihn her!		To hold him once is all I ask!
Es schling' mein Arm sich um sie her!		To hold her once is all I ask!
Und wenn es auch mein Ende wär! *(Sie umarmen sich.)*		Though just one kiss may be the last! *(They embrace.)*

Was soll das heissen? *Chorus* Are they mad?

Welch eine Dreistigkeit! Gleich auseinander! Das geht zu weit! *(Er trennt sie, kniet dann vor Sarastro nieder.)* Dein Sklave liegt zu deinen Füßen: Laß den verwegnen Frevler büßen! Bedenk, wie frech der Knabe ist! *(Er zeigt auf Papageno.)* Durch dieses seltnen Vogels List Wollt er Pamina dir entführen. Allein ich wußt' ihn auszuspüren! Du kennst mich! Meine Wachsamkeit . . .		Stop them! What impertinence! Will you add a fresh offense? *(He parts the lovers and kneels before Sarastro.)* Your slave is prostrate at your feet. This upstart's punishment I seek. Just think what brazen schemes he dared! *(indicating Papageno)* Helped by this bird, he was prepared To find the fair Pamina and steal her. But in the end could he conceal her? You know me . . . my loyalty . . .
. . . verdient, daß man ihr Lorbeer streut. He! Gebt dem Ehrenmann sogleich . . .		. . . is plain for every eye to see. Your sort of vigilance deserves . . .
Schon deine Gnade macht mich reich!		What a generous lord I serve!
. . . nur siebenundsiebenzig Sohlenstreich'.		. . . a hundred lashes for your nerve.
Ach, Herr, den Lohn verhofft' ich nicht!		How can you treat a servant so?
Nicht Dank, es ist ja meine Pflicht! *(Monostatos wird abgeführt.)*		No need for thanks. It's what I owe. *(Monostatos is led away.)*

Es lebe Sarastro, der göttliche Weise! *Chorus* Hail Sarastro! His wisdom combines
Er lohnet und strafet in ähnlichem Kreise. Both mercy and justice in our shrine!

Führt diese beiden Fremdlinge In unsern Prüfungstempel ein; Bedecket ihre Häupter dann, Sie müssen erst gereinigt sein.		Bring both strangers reverently Into our Temple to be tried. Cover their heads. They may not see. First they must be purified.

Chor
Wenn Tugend und Gerechtigkeit
Der Großen Pfad mit Ruhm bestreut,
Dann ist die Erd' ein Himmelreich,
Und Sterbliche den Göttern gleich.

Chorus
When Justice is a certainty,
And Virtue triumphs over Vice,
Then mankind will be truly free
And earth become a paradise!

ACT TWO

FIRST SCENE

Sarastro and his
priests enter in
a solemn procession.

(nach einer Pause)
Ihr eingeweihten Diener der Götter Isis und
Osiris! Mit reiner Seele erklär' ich euch, daß
unsere heutige Versammlung eine der wichtigsten
unserer Zeit ist: Tamino, ein Königssohn,
wandelt an der Pforte unseres Tempels und
will ins Heiligtum des größten Lichtes blicken.
Diesen Tugendhaften zu bewachen, ihm freund-
schaftlich die Hand zu bieten, ist heute unsere Pflicht.

Tugend!

Verschwiegenheit!

Wohltätig!—Haltet ihr ihn für würdig, so
folgt meinem Beispiel . . . Sarastro dankt euch im
Namen der Menschheit. Die Götter haben Pamina,
das sanfte, tugendhafte Mädchen, dem Jüngling bestimmt. Dies ist der Grund, warum ich sie der Mutter
entriß. Dieses Weib hofft durch Blendwerk und
Aberglauben das Volk zu berücken und unsern
festen Tempelbau zu zerstören.
Das soll sie nicht! Tamino soll ihn als
Eingeweihter mituns befestigen.
(dreimalige Akkord mit den Hörnern)

Er ist mehr! Er ist Mensch!

Man führe Tamino mit seinem Reisegefährten
in den Vorhof des Tempels ein.
(zum alten Priester, der vor ihm niederkniet)
Und du vollziehe dein heiliges Amt: Lehre sie
beide die Macht der Götter erkennen!

(after a pause)
Consecrated servants of the great gods Isis
and Osiris! With a pure heart I declare that our
gathering today is one of the weightiest of our time.
Tamino, the son of a king, waits at the gate
of our Temple, longing to be enlightened
in our sanctuary. It is our solemn
duty now to watch over this high-minded youth
and extend to him the hand of friendship.

He is.

He can.

Benevolent, yes. If you find him worthy, follow my
example . . . *(Three trumpet fanfares sound.)* Sarastro
thanks you in the name of humanity. Pamina, a pure
and gentle maiden, has been designated by the gods
for this young man. This was the reason I separated
her from her mother. That woman hopes by superstition and delusion to bewitch the people and
undermine the very foundations of our Temple.
She shall not succeed! To strengthen our cause,
Tamino himself shall become one of us.
(three trumpet blasts)

He is more! He is a man!

Let Tamino and his companion be led
into the forecourt of the Temple.
(to the Old Priest, who kneels before him)
Now fulfill your duty and teach them both
to understand the power of the gods!

Is he virtuous?

Can he keep silent?

Is he benevolent?

Besitzt er Tugend?

Auch Verschwiegenheit?

Ist wohltätig?

Great Sarastro, can Tamino survive
the ordeals that lie before him?
He is merely a prince.

We mark and marvel at your wisdom.

Großer Sarastro, wird Tamino die harten
Prüfungen, die seiner warten, bestehen?
Er ist Prinz.

Wir erkennen und verehren deine Weisheit.

Grant, Osiris and great Isis,
This noble pair your wisdom's power.
Grant your strength for every crisis,
Your light in danger's darkest hour.
O, Isis und Osiris, schenket
Der Weisheit Geist dem neuen Paar!
Die ihr der Wand'rer Schritte lenket,
Stärkt mit Geduld sie in Gefahr.

Your light in danger's darkest hour.
Stärkt mit Geduld sie in Gefahr. *Chorus*

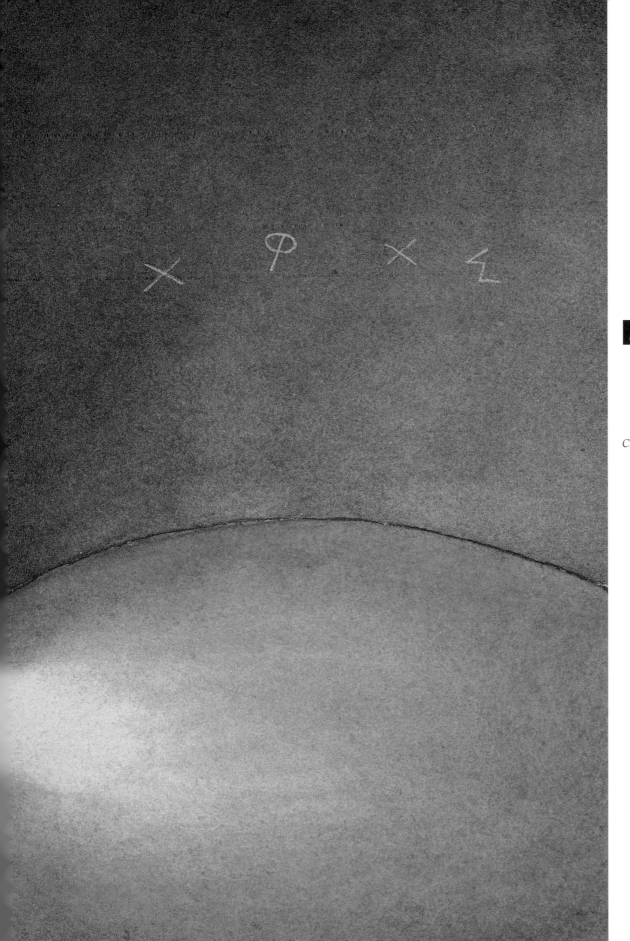

Grant they may yet conquer death
But if they fail the final test,
Find for them in heaven's breadth
A lasting peace, eternal rest.
Laßt sie der Prüfung Früchte sehen;
Doch sollten sie zu Grabe gehen,
So lohnt der Tugend kühnen Lauf,
Nehmt sie in euren Wohnsitz auf.

A lasting peace, eternal rest.

Chorus *(Sarastro leaves. The assembled Priests follow.)*
Nehmt sie in euren Wohnsitz auf.
(Sarastro geht voraus, dann alle ihm nach ab)

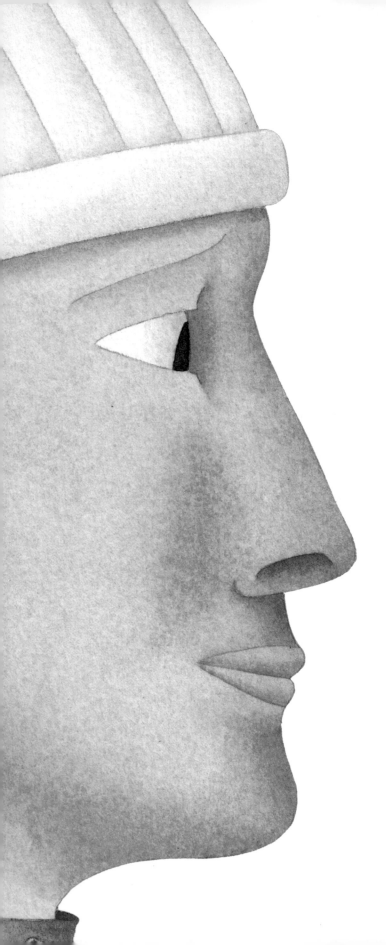

SECOND SCENE

Eine schreckliche Nacht! — Papageno,
bist du noch bei mir?

Wo denkst du, daß wir uns befinden?

Was ist's?

Du hast ja Angst, wie ich höre.

What a terrible night! — Papageno,
are you still with me?

Where do you think we are?

What's that?

You're afraid. I hear it in your voice.

Tamino and Papageno are led in by the Three Priests, who withdraw.

Sure, I'm with you!

Where? If it weren't so dark,
I could tell you, but as it is . . .
(a clap of thunder)
Oh my!

This sort of affair is not for me!

It's not my voice! There are icy
shivers up and down my back.
(a louder clap of thunder)
Oh dear!

Ja freilich!

Wo? Ja, wenn's nicht zu finster wär',
wollt' ich dir's schon sagen, aber so . . .
(Donnerschlag)
O, — O weh!

Mir wird nicht wohl bei der Sache!

Angst nicht, nur eiskalt läuft's mir
über den Rücken.
(starker Donnerschlag)
O, — O weh!

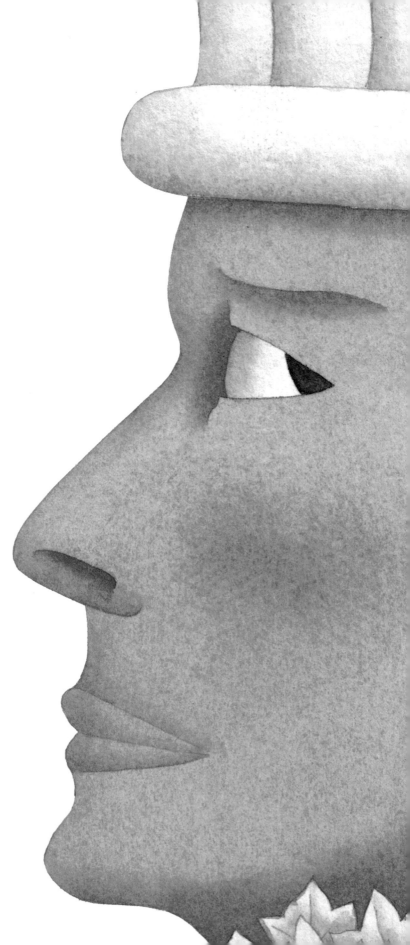

THIRD SCENE

Freundschaft und Liebe.  Friendship and love.

Ja! Yes!

Jeder! Every one!

Kämpfen ist meine Sache nicht. Ich verlange ja auch im Grunde gar keine Weisheit. Ich bin nur so ein Naturmensch, der sich mit Schlaf, Speise und Trank begnügt: und wenn es sein könnte, daß ich mir mal ein schönes Weibchen fänge . . .

Striving's not for me. To tell the truth, I don't much care for wisdom. I'm a simple man. A little sleep, a little food and drink— that's enough for me. And if I could only catch a pretty little wife for myself . . .

Worin bestehen diese Prüfungen?

What are they exactly?

Ich bleibe ledig!

I'll stay single!

Mir ganz gleich? Ist sie jung?

Exactly like me? Is she young?

Und heißt?

And her name?

Wie? Pa . . . pa . . .

What? Pa . . . Pa . . .

Papagena? Na, die möcht ich aus bloßer Neugierde sehen.

Papagena? I'd at least like to see her— just out of curiosity.

Aber wenn ich sie gesehen habe, dann muß ich sterben?—Ich bleibe ledig!

But after I've seen her I have to die?— I'll stay single!

O ja!

Oh yes!

The Two Priests return with torches.

Strangers, what brings you here within our walls?	Ihr Fremdlinge, was treibt euch an, in unsere Mauern zu dringen?
Are you prepared to risk your lives for them?	Bist du bereit, sie mit deinem Leben zu erkämpfen?
Prepared to undergo ordeals?	Du unterziehst dich jeder Prüfung?
Then give me your hand! *(Tamino grasps his hand.)*	So reiche mir deine Hand! *(Sie reichen sich die Hände.)*
Papageno, are you prepared to strive for the love of wisdom?	Willst auch du die Weisheitsliebe erkämpfen, Papageno?
That you shall never do, unless you undergo these ordeals.	Die wirst du nie erhalten, wenn du dich nicht unseren Prüfungen unterziehst.
To submit to all our commands and not to shrink even from death itself.	Dich allen unseren Gesetzen zu unterwerfen und selbst den Tod nicht zu scheuen.
And what if Sarastro has already destined a bride for you, a maiden exactly like you, down to the last feather?	Wenn nun aber Sarastro dir ein Mädchen bestimmt hätte, das an Farbe und Kleidung dir ganz gleich wäre?
Young and beautiful!	Jung und schön!
Papagena.	Papagena.
Papagena!	Papagena!
You may see her!	Sehen kannst du sie!
You may see her, but do you possess the steadfastness not to speak a word to her?	Sehen kannst du sie. Aber wirst du so viel Standhaftigkeit besitzen, kein Wort mit ihr zu sprechen?
Give me your hand! You shall see her.	Deine Hand! Du sollst sie sehen.
On you as well, Prince, the gods impose a vow of silence. You will see Pamina, but you must not speak to her! Now begins the first of your trials.	Auch dir, Prinz, legen die Götter Stillschweigen auf. Du wirst Pamina sehen, aber sie nie sprechen dürfen! Dies ist der Anfang eurer Prüfungszeit.

No.
11

Beware the wiles of womankind,
The Temple's first command insists.
Wiser men have been made blind
And yielded where they should resist.
Too late they see they've been mistaken,
Their loyalty repaid with scorn.
By all but death they are forsaken,
Betrayed, abandoned, and forlorn.
(The Two Priests leave.)
Bewahret euch vor Weibertücken:
Dies ist des Bundes erste Pflicht!
Manch weiser Mann ließ sich berücken,
Er fehlte und versah sich's nicht.
Verlassen sah er sich am Ende,
Vergolten seine Treu mit Hohn!
Vergebens rang er seine Hände,
Tod und Verzweiflung war sein Lohn.
(beide Priester ab)

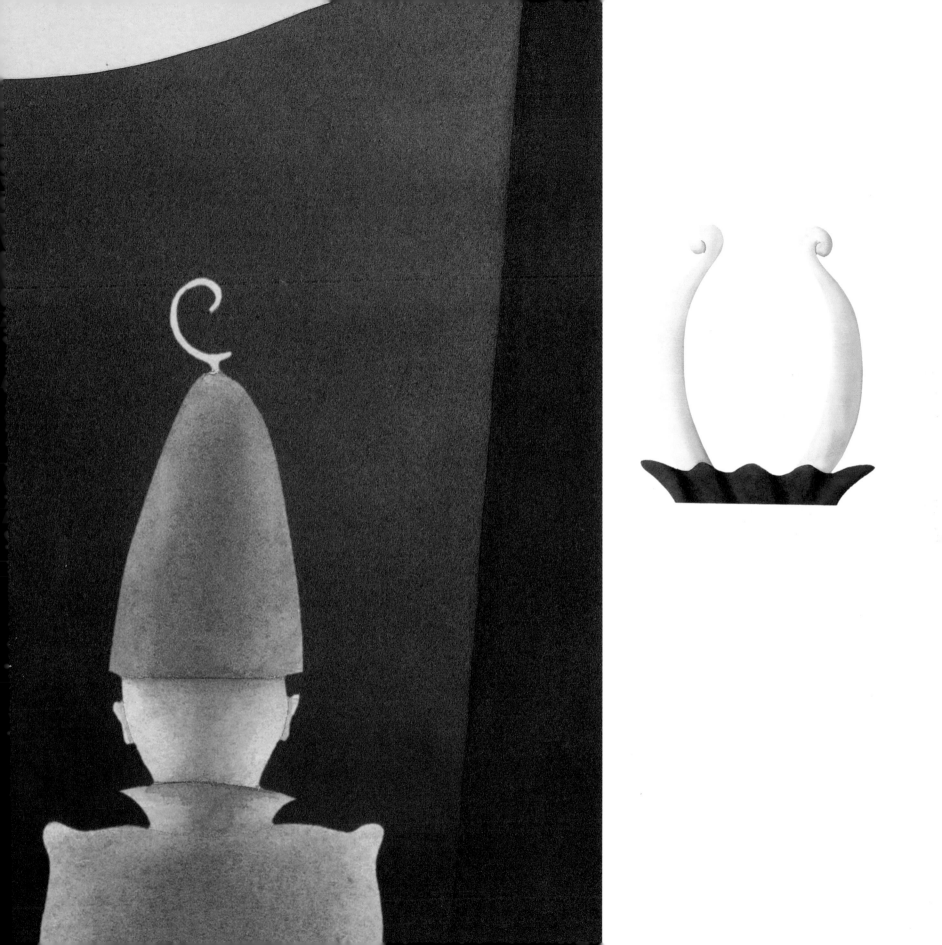

FOURTH SCENE

Tamino and
Papageno alone.
Darkness.

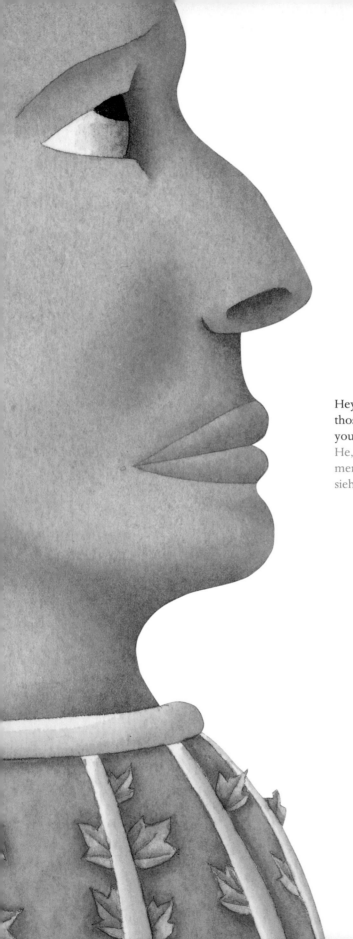

Hey! Some light here! It's strange—every time
those men leave you can't see a thing, even with
your eyes wide open.
He, Lichter her! Lichter her! S'ist doch
merk-würdig: so oft einen die Herren verlassen,
sieht man mit offenen Augen nichts mehr!

Bear it with patience, and remember
it is the will of the gods.
Ertrag es mit Geduld und denke,
es ist der Götter Wille.

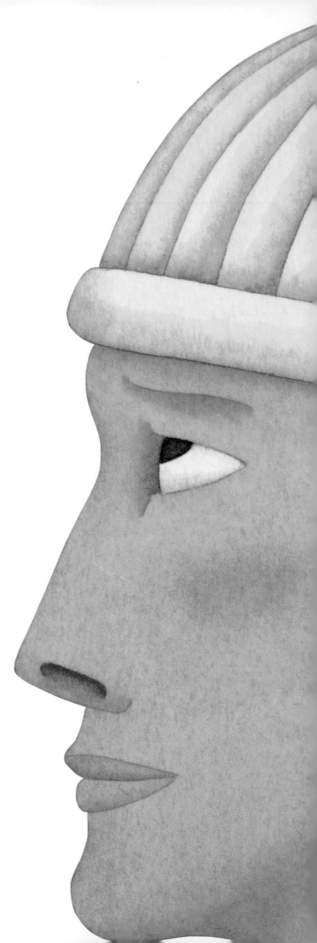

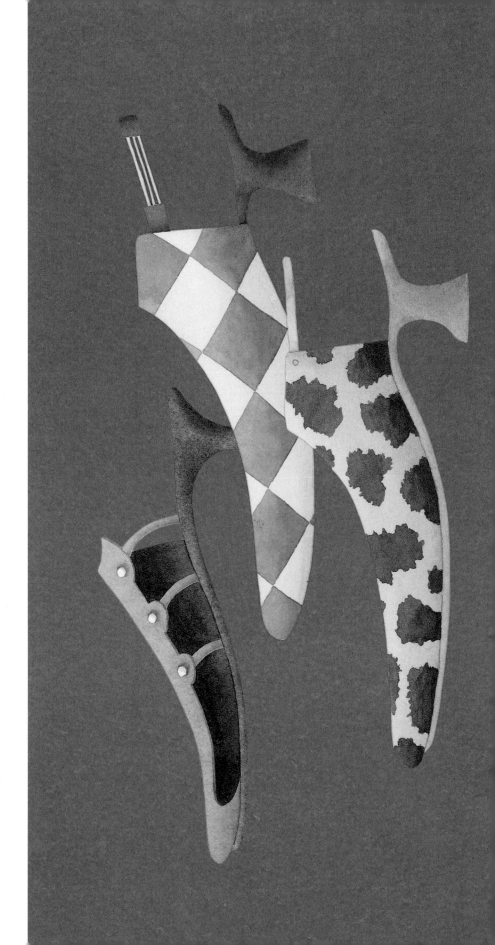

FIFTH SCENE

The Three Ladies
suddenly appear.

Wie? Wie? Wie?	Why? Why? Why
Ihr an diesem Schreckensort?	Stay amid such dark and gloom?
Nie, nie, nie	Fly! Fly! Fly
Kommt ihr glücklich	For fear you meet a
wieder fort!	gruesome doom!
Tamino, dir ist	Tamino, you are now
Tod geschworen!	death's pawn!
Du, Papageno, bist verloren!	For Papageno, all hope's gone!

Nein, nein, nein! Das wär' zu viel!		No, no, no! This is all too much!
Papageno, schweige still! Willst du dein Gelübde brechen, Nichts mit Weibern hier zu sprechen?		Papageno, hold your tongue! Have you so soon forgotten your vow? Words with women are not allowed.
Du hörst ja, wir sind beide hin.		Haven't you heard? We're both done for!
Stille, sag ich! Schweige still!		Silence, I said! Not one word more!
Immer still und immer still!		Agreed, agreed. Not one word more.
Ganz nah ist euch die Königin! Sie drang im Tempel heimlich ein.		But now the Queen herself is near! In secrecy she has come here!
Wie? Was? Sie soll im Tempel sein?		What? The Queen herself's appeared?
Stille, sag ich! Schweige still! Wirst du immer so vermessen Deiner Eidespflicht vergessen?		Silence, I said! Not one word more! I've scolded your impudence before. Remember the solemn oath you swore.
Tamino, hör! Du bist verloren! Gedenke an die Königin! Man zischelt viel sich in die Ohren Von dieser Priester falschem Sinn.		Tamino, listen! You are doomed! Think now only of the Queen! People whisper. They assume That nothing here is what it seems.
(für sich) Ein Weiser prüft und achtet nicht, was der gemeine Pöbel spricht.		*(aside)* A truly wise man's not deceived By gossip only fools believe.
Man sagt, wer ihrem Bunde schwört, Der fährt zur Höll' mit Haut und Haar.	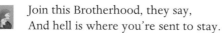	Join this Brotherhood, they say, And hell is where you're sent to stay.

Now what the devil am I to do?
Tell me, Tamino, is it true?
Das wär' beim Teufel unerhört!
Sag an, Tamino, ist das wahr?

The idle tales old wives repeat
Are filled with drivel and deceit.
Geschwätz, von Weibern nachgesagt,
Von Heuchlern aber ausgedacht.

The Queen herself has said it's true.
She thinks as other women do.
Doch sagt es auch die Königin.
Sie ist ein Weib, hat Weibersinn.

Stay silent now, and trust my word.
Your vow comes first, not what you've heard.
Sei still, mein Wort sei dir genug,
Denk deiner Pflicht und handle klug.

(to Tamino)
Is prudishness a frank reply?
(zu Tamino)
Warum bist du mit uns so spröde?

(He indicates he dare not speak.)
(Er deutet an, daß er nicht sprechen darf.)

And Papageno silent? Why?
Auch Papageno schweigt—so rede!

(secretly, to the Ladies)
I'd gladly speak . . . I wish . . .
(heimlich zu den Damen)
Ich möchte gerne . . . woll . . .

Hush!
Still!

As you see, I'm not . . .
Ihr seht, daß ich nicht soll . . .

Hush!
Still!

My blithering, babbling tongue's to blame,
And I should truly be ashamed.
Daß ich nicht kann das Plaudern lassen,
Ist wahrlich eine Schand für mich!

Your blithering, babbling tongue's to blame.
Yes, you should truly be ashamed!
Daß du nicht kannst das Plaudern lassen,
Ist wahrlich eine Schand für dich!

In shame we must depart at last.
Their vow of silence holds steadfast.
Wir müssen sie mit Scham verlassen,
Es plaudert keiner sicherlich.

In shame they should depart at last.
Our vow of silence holds steadfast!
Sie müssen uns mit Scham verlassen,
Es plaudert keiner sicherlich.

All
This proves the ways of women weak.
Men will think before they speak.
Von festem Geiste ist ein Mann,
Er denket, was er sprechen kann.

(from within)
These women are to be reviled!
Our sacred Temple is defiled!
(von innen)
Entweiht ist die heilige Schwelle!
Hinab mit den Weibern zur Hölle!

Away!
(In a thundering darkness,
they vanish out of sight.)
O weh!
(Die Damen stürzen in die Versenkung.)

Alas!
(He falls to the ground.)
O weh!
(Er fällt zu Boden.)

SIXTH SCENE

Tamino! Dein standhaft männliches Betragen hat gesiegt. Aber du hast noch manchen gefährlichen Weg zu wandern! Komm! Komm!

(zu Papageno)
Papageno, steh auf!

Auf! Sei ein Mann!

Komm! Ich führe dich weiter!

Tamino! Your steadfast, manly bearing has won the day. But many perilous paths still lie ahead! Come!

(to Papageno)
Papageno, stand up!

Up! Be a man!

Come! I'll lead you farther on!

The Two Priests enter.

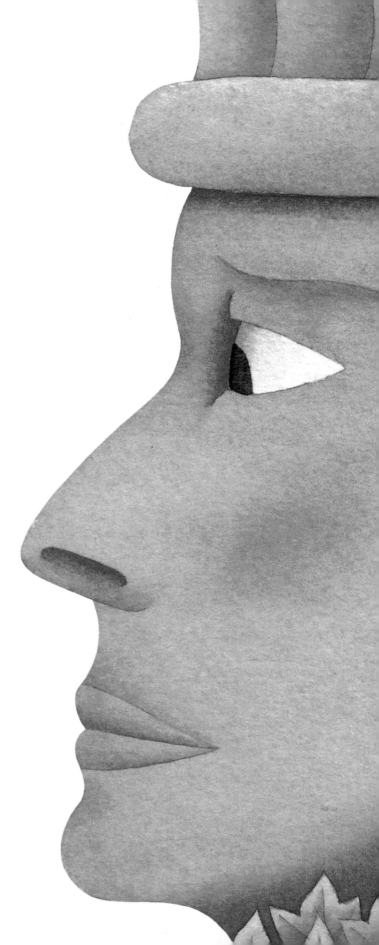

I fainted dead away!

If the gods have already promised me a Papagena, why do I have to go through so many dangers to find her?

In all this endless wandering, a man could fall out of love forever.

Ich lieg' in einer Ohnmacht.

Aber wenn mir die Götter eine Papagena bestimmten, warum muß ich sie dann mit soviel Gefahren erringen?

Bei so einer ewigen Wanderschaft könnte einem wohl die Liebe auf immer vergehen.

SEVENTH SCENE

A garden where
Pamina is sleeping.
Monostatos is
watching her.

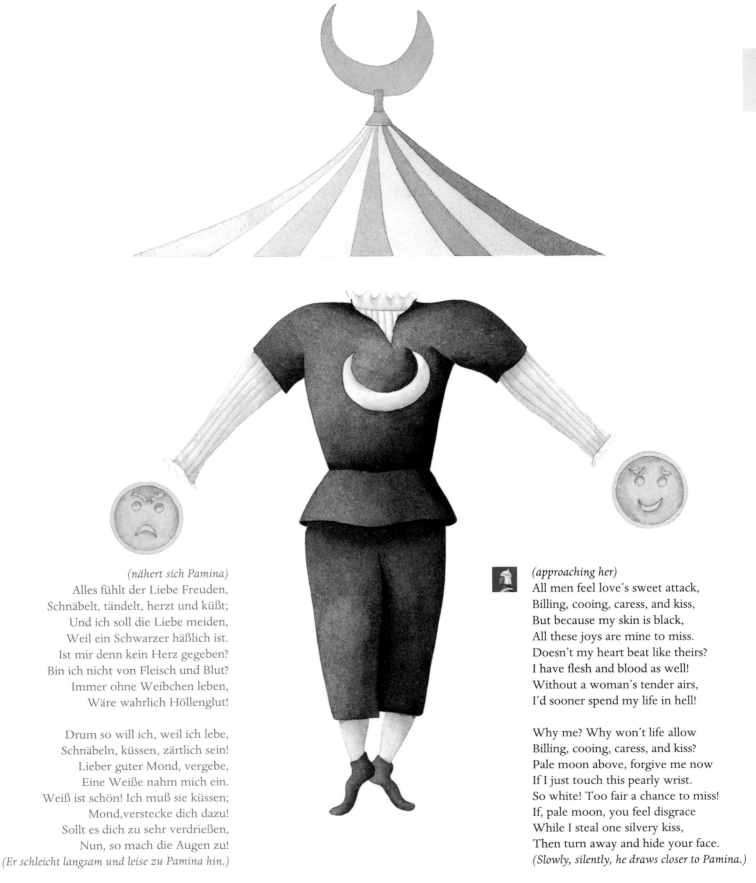

(nähert sich Pamina)
Alles fühlt der Liebe Freuden,
Schnäbelt, tändelt, herzt und küßt;
Und ich soll die Liebe meiden,
Weil ein Schwarzer häßlich ist.
Ist mir denn kein Herz gegeben?
Bin ich nicht von Fleisch und Blut?
Immer ohne Weibchen leben,
Wäre wahrlich Höllenglut!

Drum so will ich, weil ich lebe,
Schnäbeln, küssen, zärtlich sein!
Lieber guter Mond, vergebe,
Eine Weiße nahm mich ein.
Weiß ist schön! Ich muß sie küssen;
Mond, verstecke dich dazu!
Sollt es dich zu sehr verdrießen,
Nun, so mach die Augen zu!
(Er schleicht langsam und leise zu Pamina hin.)

(approaching her)
All men feel love's sweet attack,
Billing, cooing, caress, and kiss,
But because my skin is black,
All these joys are mine to miss.
Doesn't my heart beat like theirs?
I have flesh and blood as well!
Without a woman's tender airs,
I'd sooner spend my life in hell!

Why me? Why won't life allow
Billing, cooing, caress, and kiss?
Pale moon above, forgive me now
If I just touch this pearly wrist.
So white! Too fair a chance to miss!
If, pale moon, you feel disgrace
While I steal one silvery kiss,
Then turn away and hide your face.
(Slowly, silently, he draws closer to Pamina.)

EIGHTH SCENE

Zurücke	Stand back!

Ach! Das ist . . . die Königin der Nacht.		Alas! This is . . . the Queen of the Night!
Mutter? . . . Das muß ich belauschen.		Mother? This I should watch from afar.

Wo ist der Jüngling, den ich an dich sandte?

Where is the young man I sent to you?

Dann ist er verloren. Siehst du hier diesen Stahl?
 Er ist für Sarastro geschliffen.
 Du wirst ihn töten...

Then he is doomed. Do you see this dagger?
 It has been sharpened for Sarastro.
 It is for you to kill him . . .

. . . und den mächtigen Sonnenkreis mir überliefern.

. . . and deliver to me the great Circle of the Sun.

Amid thunder, the Queen appears.

(awakening)
Mother!

Mother! My own!

He has sworn himself to the Brotherhood.

Mother!

(erwacht)
Mutter!

Mutter! Meine Mutter!

Er hat sich den Eingeweihten gewidmet.

Mutter!

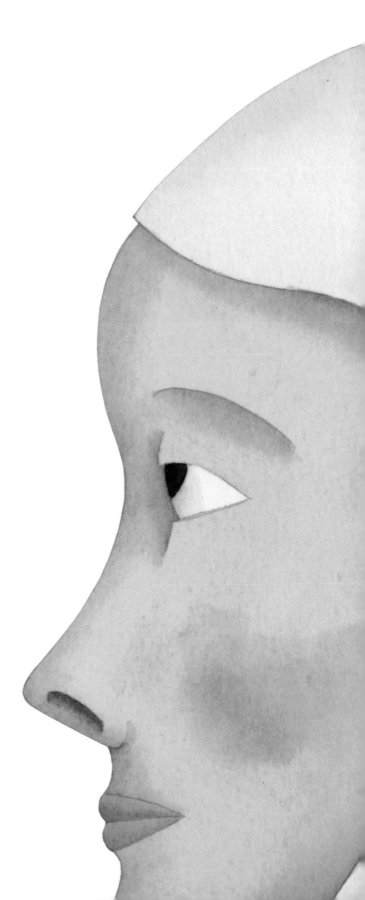

Hell's blood surges through my breast,
Despair and death now blind my eyes!
You'll plunge this knife into his chest
Or forever after agonize.
No more my daughter! Outcast! Alone!
Unless Sarastro dies, the worst
Will harrow you. You'll be disowned!
Hear, vengeful gods, a mother's curse!
(Amid loud thunder, she disappears.)

Der Hölle Rache kocht in meinem Herzen,
Tod und Verzweiflung flammet um mich her!
Fühlt nicht durch dich Sarastro Todesschmerzen.
So bist du meine Tochter nimmermehr.
Verstoßen sei auf ewig, verlassen sei auf ewig,
Zertrümmert sei'n auf ewig alle Bande der Natur,
Wenn nicht durch dich Sarastro wird erblassen!
Hört! Rachegötter! Hört der Mutter Schwur!
(sie versinkt)

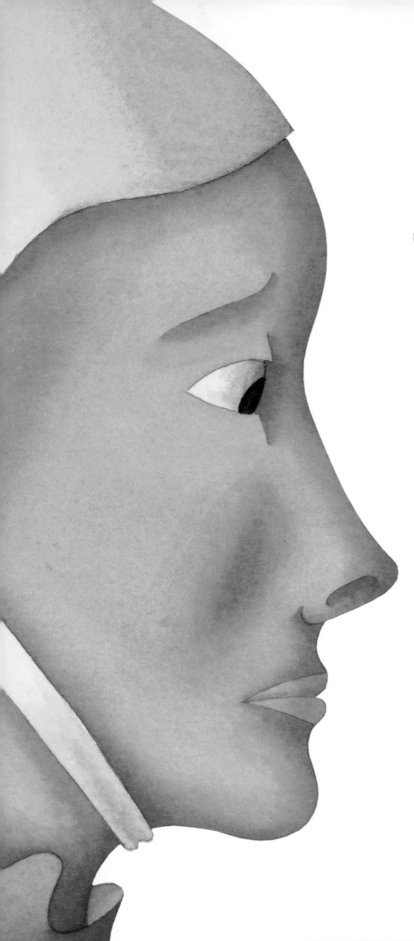

NINTH SCENE

Morden soll ich?—Das kann ich nicht!

Murder him? I cannot do it!

TENTH SCENE

. . . Götter! Was soll ich tun?

. . . Heavens! What shall I do?

Dir? Gib mir den Dolch zurück!

To you? Give the dagger back to me!

Der wäre?

What way?

Götter!

Gods!

Nein! Nie!

No! Never!

Pamina with the dagger in her hand.
Monostatos returns.

Monostatos approaches the girl.

Trust yourself to me!
(He takes the dagger from her.)

Now there is just one way to
save your mother and yourself.

By loving me!

Which is it then, yes or no?

Dich mir anvertrauen!
(nimmt ihr den Dolch weg)

Du hast also nur einen Weg,
dich und deine Mutter zu retten.

Mich zu lieben!

Nun, Mädchen! Ja oder nein!

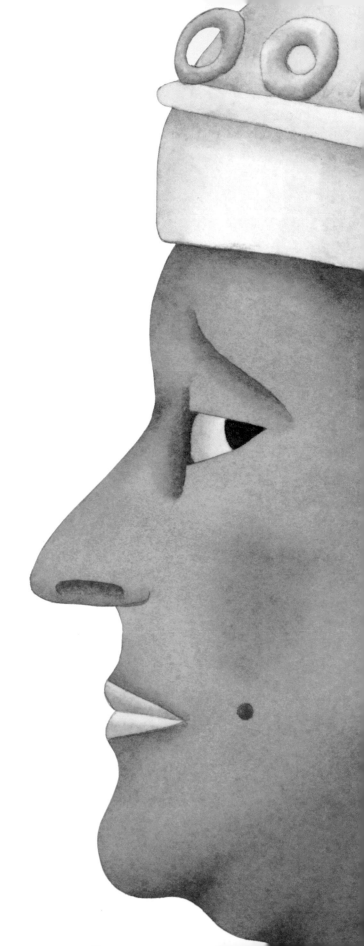

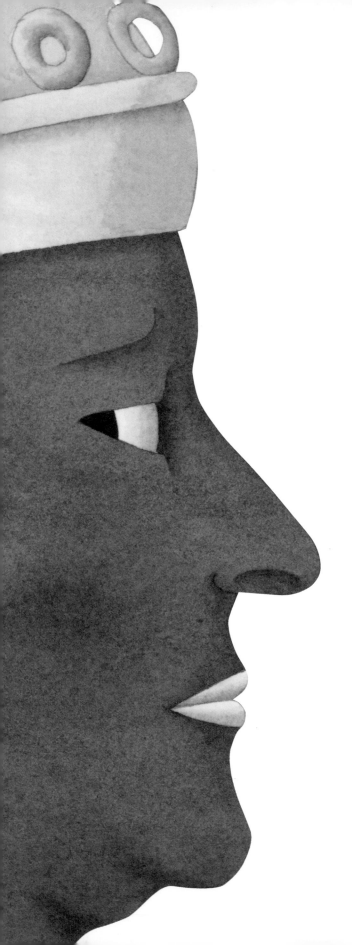

ELEVENTH SCENE

So fahre denn hin!

Then die!

Herr, ich bin unschuldig! Man wollte dich töten!
Ich wollte dich rächen.

My lord, I am innocent! They wanted to murder
you! I wanted only to avenge you!

TWELFTH SCENE

Herr! Strafe meine Mutter nicht,
der Schmerz, mich zu verlieren . . .

 Lord, Do not punish my mother!
Her grief at losing me . . .

Sarastro enters.

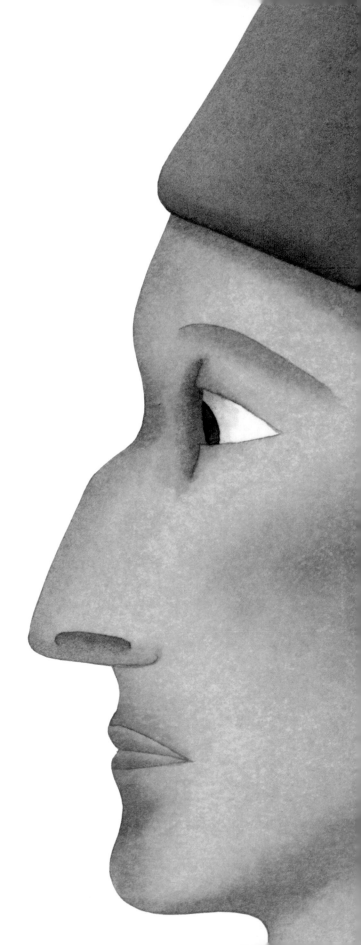

Get back!

Zurück!

I know, I know everything. Go!
(*Monostatos flees.*)

Ich weiß, ich weiß alles! Geh!
(*Monostatos entflieht.*)

Pamina and Sarastro.

Be calm! You shall see how I take vengeance on your mother.

Sei ruhig! Du sollst sehen, wie ich mich an deiner Mutter räche.

In diesen heil'gen Hallen
Kennt man die Rache nicht,
Und ist ein Mensch gefallen,
Führt Liebe ihn zur Pflicht.
Dann wandelt er an Freundes Hand
Vergnügt und froh ins bess're Land.

 Within these sacred halls
Revenge remains unknown.
And if a man should fall,
His way by love is shown.
And gently led by friendship's hand,
He's guided to a better land.

In diesen heil'gen Mauern,
Wo Mensch den Menschen liebt,
Kann kein Verräter lauern,
Weil man dem Feind vergibt.
Wen solche Lehren nicht erfreun,
Verdienet nicht, ein Mensch zu sein.
(Beide gehen ab.)

Within these sacred walls
By love do all men live,
No treachery befalls.
Our enemies we forgive.
Those who scorn our noble plan
Do not deserve the name of man.
(They depart.)

THIRTEENTH
SCENE

A great hall. Tamino
and Papageno are led in
by the Two Priests.

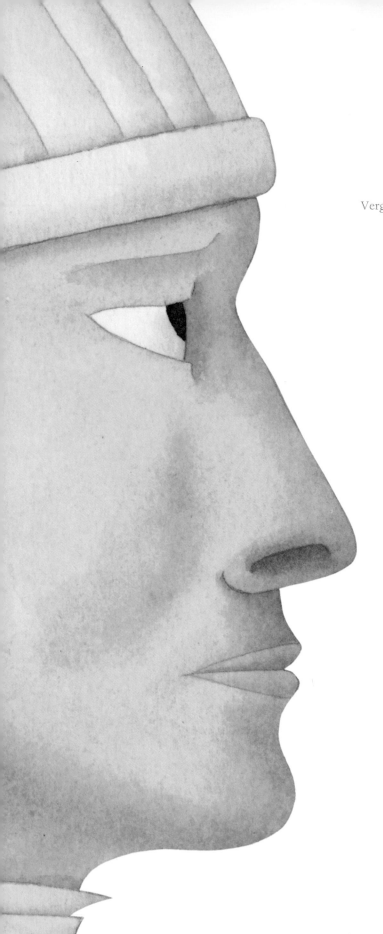

Hier seid ihr beide euch allein überlassen.
Vergeßt das Wort nicht: Schweigen. Lebt wohl!
(Die Priester entfernen sich.)

 Here you shall both be left alone. Be
mindful of one word: silence! Farewell!
(The Priests depart.)

FOURTEENTH SCENE

(verweisend)
St!

(silencing him)
Shh!

(verweisend)
St!

(silencing him)
Shh!

St!

Shh!

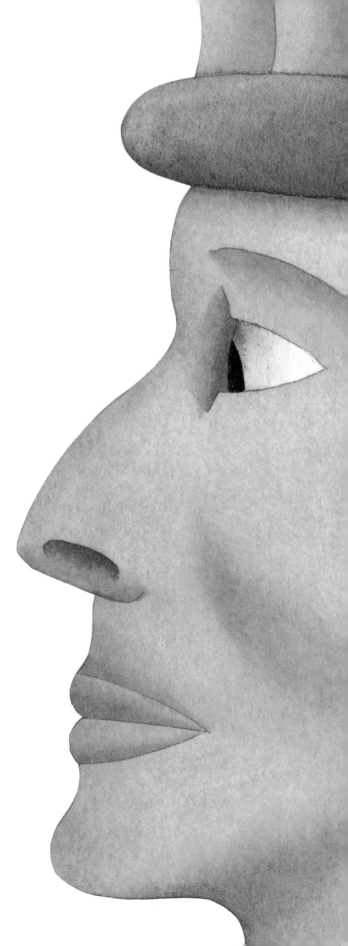

Tamino and Papageno are left alone.

(after a pause)
Tamino!

Isn't this the life! If I were back in my straw hut,
or in the forest, at least I'd hear a bird sing.

Surely I'm allowed to talk to myself.
And why can't we speak just to each other,
man to man?

La la la—la la la!
These people won't even give us a drop of water,
much less anything else.

(nach einer Pause)
Tamino!

Das ist ein lustiges Leben! Wär' ich doch in
meiner Strohhütte, oder im Wald, hört' ich
wenigstens manchmal einen Vogel pfeifen!

Na, mit mir selbst werd' ich doch wohl sprechen
dürfen; und auch wir zwei können zusammen
sprechen, wir sind ja Männer.

La la la—la la la!
Nicht einmal einen Tropfen Wasser bekommt
man bei diesen Leuten, viel weniger sonst was.

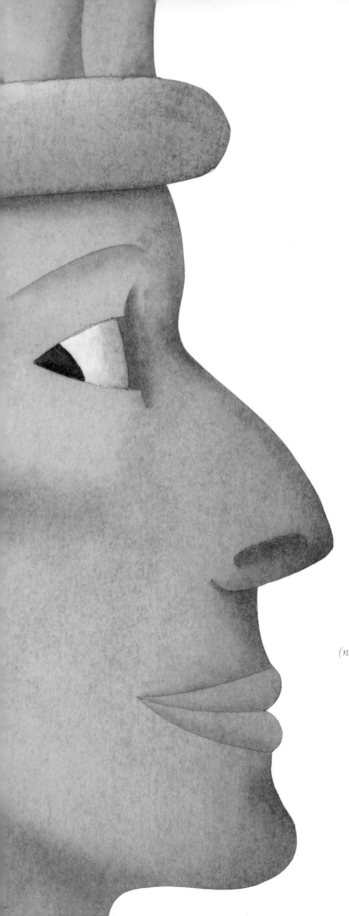

FIFTEENTH SCENE

Ja, wer kommt denn da?	Who goes there?
He, du Alte!	Hey, old lady!
Ist dieser Becher für mich?	Is that cup for me?
(er trinkt)	*(drinking)*
Prrrrr . . . Wasser!	Ahh! . . . Water!
So, So!	Well, well!
Geh, Alte, setz dich her zu mir, mir ist die Zeit	Come, granny, sit here by me. The time passes
verdammt lang. Wie alt bist du denn?	so slowly. Tell me, how old are you?
Achtzig Jahr und zwei Minuten?	Eighty years and two minutes?
Achtzehn Jahr und zwei Minuten! Hahahahaha!	Eighteen years and two minutes! Ha, ha!
Du junger Engel! Hast du auch einen Geliebten?	My little angel! And have you a sweetheart?
Ist er auch so jung wie du?	And is he as young as you?
Um zehn Jahre ist er älter als du?	Ten years older than you?
Na, das muß eine Liebe sein.	Now, that must be love indeed!
Wie nennt sich denn dein Liebhaber?	And what is your sweetheart's name?
Papageno? Wo ist er denn, dieser Papageno?	Papageno? Where is he then, this Papageno?
Ich wäre dein Geliebter?	What, me your sweetheart?
(nimmt schnell das Wasser und spritzt es ihr ins Gesicht)	*(He takes the cup and flings water in her face.)*
Sag mir, wie du heißt?!	Tell me your name!
Weg ist sie! Nun sprech ich kein Wort mehr!	She's gone! Now I won't speak another word!

An ugly old woman enters holding a large goblet of water.

It is, my angel!	Ja, mein Engel!
Yes indeed, my angel!	Freilich, mein Engel!
Eighteen years and two minutes.	Achtzehn Jahr und zwei Minuten.
Eighteen years and two minutes!	*Achtzehn* Jahr und zwei Minuten!
Me? Indeed I do!	Ich? Freilich!
Not quite. He is ten years older.	Nicht ganz, er ist um zehn Jahre älter.
Papageno!	Papageno!
Sitting beside me, my angel!	Da sitzt er, mein Engel!
You, my angel!	Ja, mein Engel!
My name is . . . *(Thunder. The old woman hobbles quickly away.)*	Ich heiße! . . . *(Die Alte hinkt schnell ab.)*

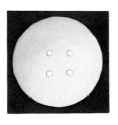

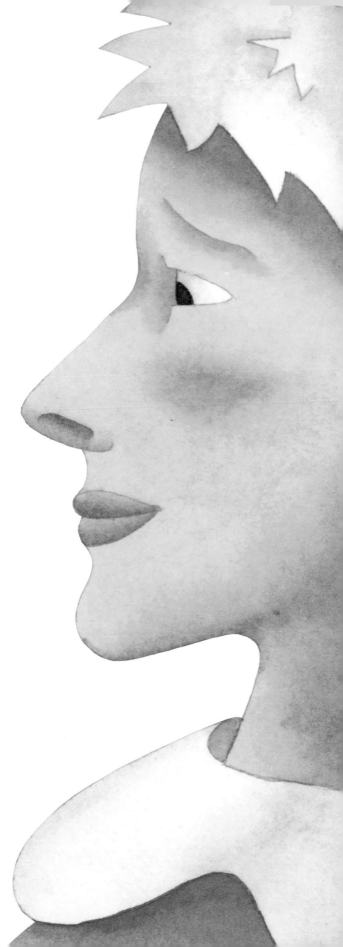

No.
16

SIXTEENTH
SCENE

The Three Spirits
enter. One carries
the magic flute,
another the chimes.

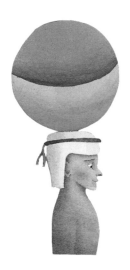

Welcome, strangers, a second time.
It's here that great Sarastro dwells.
At his command, you now will find
Your magic flute, your magic bells.
(A table with food and drink mysteriously appears.)
This tasty feast we now provide you.
So eat and drink, and have no fear.
When next we three shall stand beside you,
You both will find rewards are near.
Close by, Tamino, is she you seek.
And Papageno—do not speak!
(They withdraw.)

Seid uns zum zweiten Mal willkommen,
Ihr Männer, in Sarastros Reich.
Er schickt, was man euch abgenommen,
Die Flöte und die Glöckchen euch.
(Ein Tisch mit Speise und Trank erscheint.)
Wollt ihr die Speisen nicht verschmähen,
So esset, trinket froh davon.
Wenn wir zum drittenmal uns sehen,
Ist Freude eures Mutes Lohn!
Tamino, Mut! Nah ist das Ziel.
Du, Papageno, schweige still!
(Sie verschwinden.)

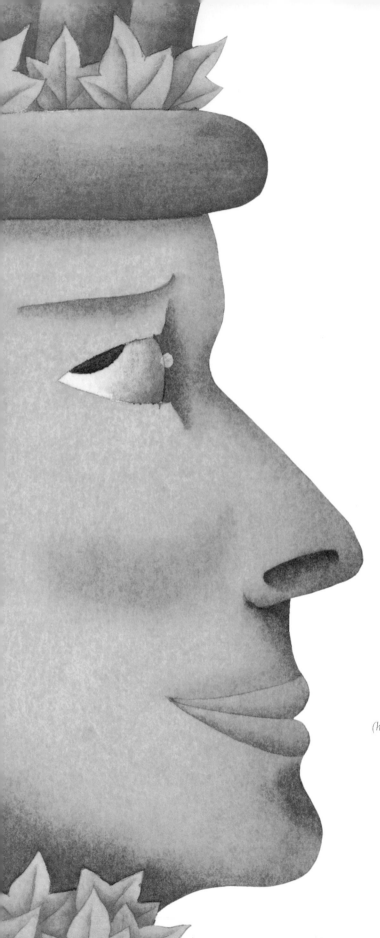

SEVENTEENTH SCENE

Tamino, wollen wir nicht speisen?	Tamino, shouldn't we eat something?
(Tamino bläst auf seiner Flöte.)	*(Tamino plays his flute.)*
Blas du nur fort auf deiner Flöte!	So play away on that flute!
Hm . . . Ah! Sarastro führt eine gute Küche.	Mmm, Sarastro sure has sent us a feast.
Ich will schon schweigen,	I'd happily stay silent
wenn ich immer so gute Bissen bekomme.	if there were always such things to eat.
Ob auch der Keller so gut bestellt ist?	Let's see if his cellar is as good as his kitchen.
Ah! – Ein Götterwein!	Ahh!—what heavenly wine!
(Die Flöte schweigt.)	*(The flute stops playing.)*

EIGHTEENTH SCENE

(hat einen Brocken im Munde, winkt fortzugehen)	*(His mouth full of food, he too motions her to go away.)*
Hm! hm! hm!	Hm, hm, hm!

Tamino and Papageno alone.

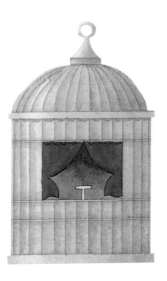

Pamina enters.

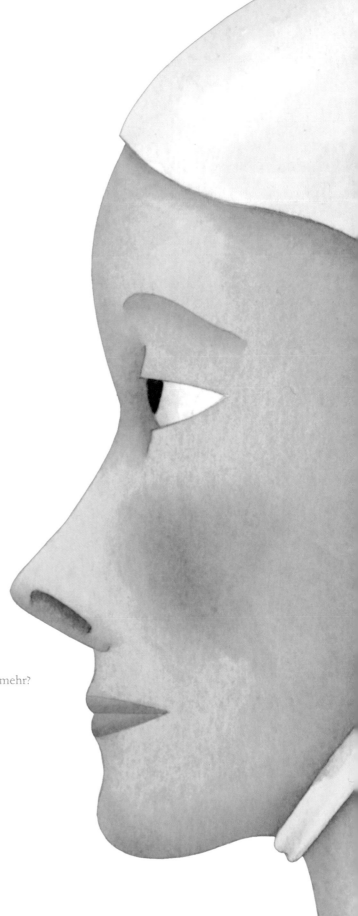

(joyfully)
Tamino! You here! I heard your flute and ran
toward the sound. But . . . you look sad.
Not even a word for your Pamina?
(Tamino motions to her to go away.)
What? Leave you? Do you no longer love me?
Papageno, tell me, what is troubling him?

My beloved Tamino!
Oh, this is worse than death itself!

(freudig)
Tamino! Du hier? Ich hörte deine Flöte und lief
dem Tone nach. Aber . . . du bist traurig?
Sprichst nicht eine Silbe mit deiner Pamina?
(Tamino winkt ihr fortzugehen.)
Wie? Ich soll dich meiden? Liebst du mich nicht mehr?
Papageno, sag du mir, was ist mit ihm?

Liebster, einziger Tamino!
Oh, das ist mehr als Tod!

I feel it now! The empty sadness!
Gone forever love's delight!
Gone forever joy and gladness!
Every brightness turned to night!
Look, Tamino, see these tears
Shed in grief for you, my own!
If your love should disappear,
The friend who's left is Death alone.
(Slowly she leaves.)

Ach, ich fühl's, es ist verschwunden,
Ewig hin der Liebe Glück!
Nimmer kommt ihr Wonnestunden
Meinem Herzen mehr zurück!
Sieh, Tamino, diese Tränen
Fließen, Trauter, dir allein.
Fühlst du nicht der Liebe Sehnen,
So wird Ruh' im Tode sein!
(langsam ab)

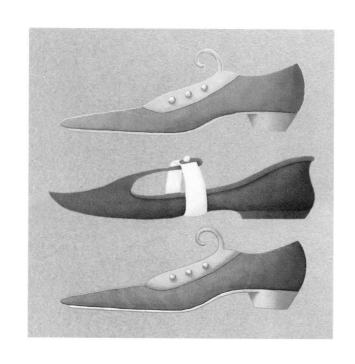

NINETEENTH
SCENE

An immense vault.
Sarastro and
his priests enter.

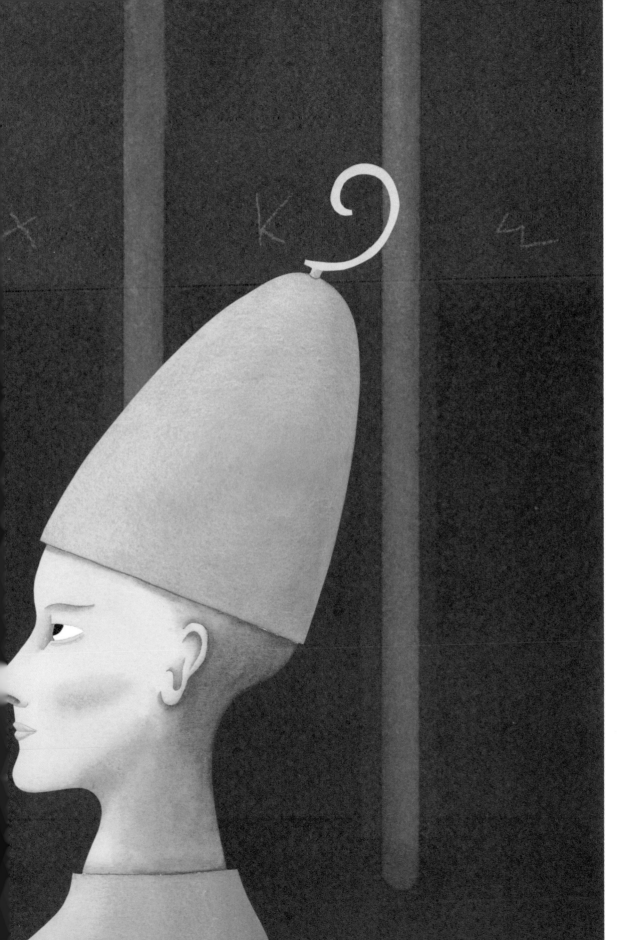

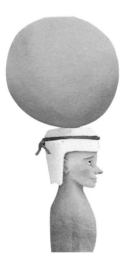

O Isis and Osiris! The light!
The sun has banished darkest night!
Soon this youth will know the good,
Soon be part of our Brotherhood.
His spirit is bold, his heart is pure.
Soon his worthiness is assured.

O, Isis und Osiris, welche Wonne!
Die düstre Nacht verscheucht der Glanz der Sonne,
Bald fühlt der edle Jüngling neues Leben;
Bald ist er unserm Dienste ganz ergeben.
Sein Geist ist kühn, sein Herz ist rein,
Bald wird er unser würdig sein.

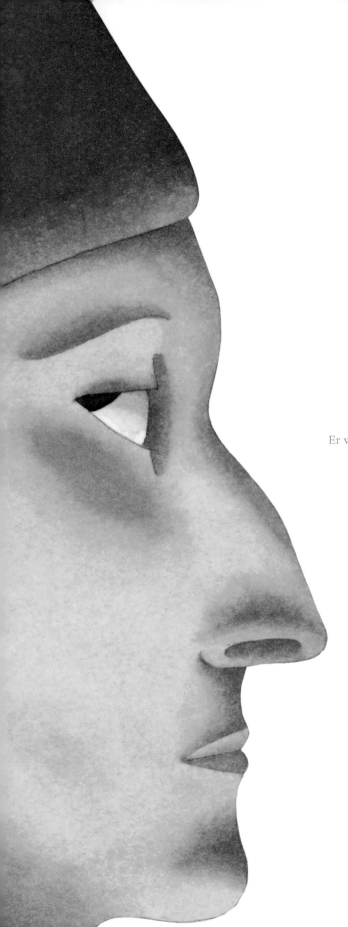

TWENTIETH SCENE

Tamino, dein Betragen war bisher männlich
und gelassen; nun hast du noch zwei gefährliche
Wege zu wandern.—Mögen die Götter
dich begleiten.—
Man bringe Pamina!
(Pamina wird hereingeführt.)
Gib mir deine Hand, Pamina!

Er wartet deiner, um dir das letze Lebewohl zu sagen.

Hier!

Zurück!

Tamino, your conduct so far has been
manly and patient.
Now you have two perilous paths still to go.
May the gods go with you—
Bring Pamina forward!
(She is brought in.)
Give me your hand, Pamina!

He awaits you—to bid a last farewell.

Here!

Stay back!

Tamino is led in by priests.
Later, Pamina is brought in too.

Where am I?	Wo bin ich?
Where is Tamino?	Wo ist Tamino?
A last farewell?	Das letzte Lebewohl!
Where is he?	Wo ist er?
Tamino!	Tamino!

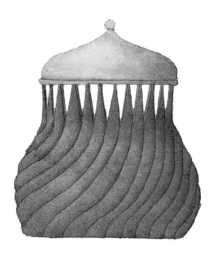

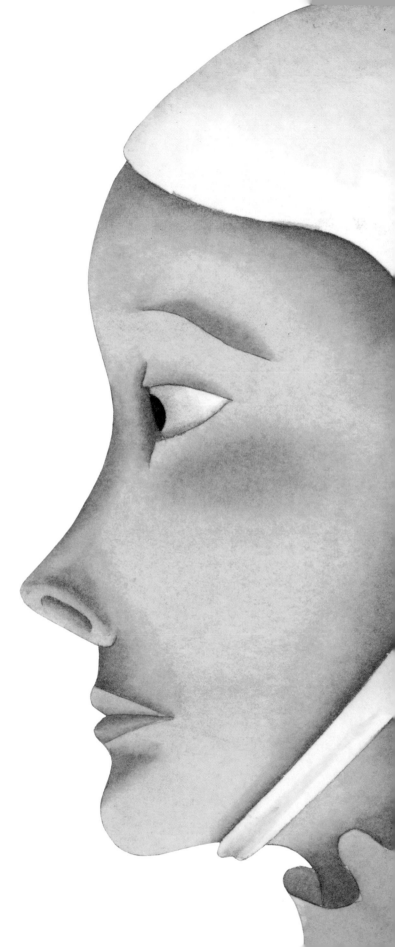

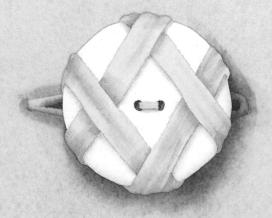

Why now, beloved, must we part?
Soll ich dich, Teurer, nicht mehr sehn?

You'll meet again with joyful hearts.
Ihr werdet froh euch wiedersehn.

But deadly dangers lie ahead!
Dein warten tödliche Gefahren!

The gods will protect me from every dread.
Die Götter mögen mich bewahren!

The gods will protect him from every dread!
Die Gotter mögen ihn bewahren!

Something whispers inside my heart
That certain death awaits you there.
Du wirst dem Tode nicht entgehen;
Mir flüstert dieses Ahnung ein.

A hidden destiny will play its part.
What fate decrees, we all must bear.
Der Götter Wille mag geschehen,
Ihr Wink soll mir (ihm) Gesetze sein.

If only you loved as I love you!
You have the feelings of a stone!
O liebtest du, wie ich dich liebe,
Du würdest nicht so ruhig sein.

Believe me, he feels the ache like you.
His heart is yours and yours alone.
Glaub mir, er fühlet gleiche Triebe,
Wird ewig dein Getreuer sein.

Believe me, I feel the ache like you.
My heart is yours and yours alone!
Glaub mir, ich fühle gleiche Triebe,
Werd' ewig dein Getreuer sein!

The hour has come, you must now part.
Die Stunde schlägt, nun müßt ihr scheiden.

This bitter moment pierces my heart.
Wie bitter sind der Trennung Leiden!

Tamino, it is time to go.
Tamino muß nun wieder fort.

Pamina, it is time I go!
Pamina, ich muß wirklich fort!

Tamino, oh must you go?
Tamino muß nun wirklich fort?

Now you must go.
Nun muß er fort.

Now I must go.
Nun muß ich fort.

Oh must you go?
So mußt du fort?

Pamina, farewell!
Pamina, lebe wohl!

Tamino, farewell!
Tamino, lebe wohl!

On your way!
Your vow summons you.
The hour strikes. We will meet again.
Nun eile fort.
Dich ruft dein Wort.
Die Stunde schlägt, wir sehn uns wieder.

May our golden rapture come again!
Farewell! Farewell!
(Sarastro withdraws with Tamino.
Pamina is led away by two priests.)
Ach, goldne Ruhe, kehre wieder!
Lebe wohl, lebe wohl!
(Sie entfernen sich.)

· 157 ·

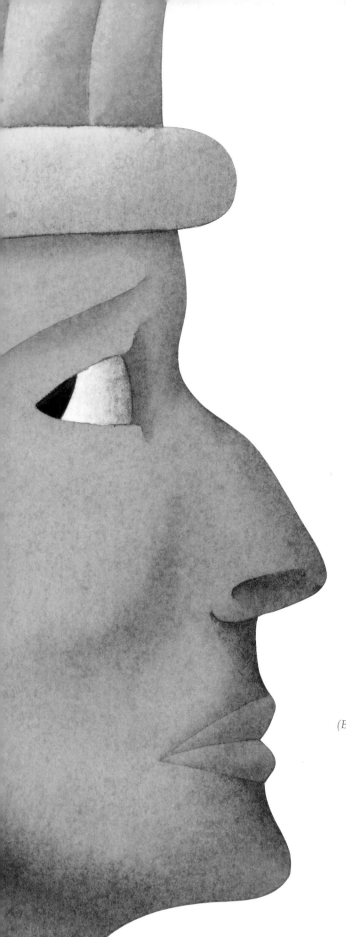

TWENTY-FIRST SCENE

(eilt ihnen nach)
Tamino! Tamino!
Willst du mich denn gänzlich verlassen?
(versucht ihnen zu folgen)
Wenn ich nur wenigstens wüßte, wo ich wäre!
(Er kommt an die Tür,
wo Tamino abgeführt worden ist.)

(following after them)
Tamino! Tamino!
Are you leaving me all alone?
(searching)
If I only knew where I was.
(He comes to the door through which
Tamino has just been led away.)

Barmherzige Götter! Wenn ich nur
wüßte, wo ich hereinkam!
(Er kommt an die Tür, wo er hereinkam.)

Merciful gods! If only I could remember
which door it was I came in.
(He goes up to the door through which he first entered.)

Nun kann ich weder vorwärts noch zurück!
Muß vielleicht am Ende gar verhungern . . .
(Er weint.)

I can't go one way or the other.
Perhaps I'm just meant to starve to death . . .
(He weeps.)

TWENTY-SECOND SCENE

Je nun, es gibt ja noch mehr Leute meines-
gleichen.—Mir wäre jetzt ein gutes Glas Wein
das himmlischste Vergnügen!
(Ein grosser Becher mit rotem Wein kommt aus der Erde.)
. . . da ist er schon, der Wein!

Well, there are plenty of chaps like me.
For me, a glass of wine right now would be
exalted enough.
(A large goblet of wine instantly appears.)
. . . and here it is, the wine!

Oh, dieser Wein ist göttlich!
Mir wird ganz wunderlich ums Herz. Ich bin
jetzt so vergnügt, dass ich bis zur Sonne fliegen
wollte, wenn ich Flügel hätte.
Ich möchte . . . ich wünschte . . .
Ja, was möcht ich denn?

This wine is heavenly!
I have this strange sensation around my heart.
I feel so good now I could fly up to the sun
if only I had wings!
I want . . . I'd like to . . .
Now what could it have been?

Papageno is left alone, as darkness falls.

(voice within)
Stand back!

(eine Stimme)
Zurück!

(voice within)
Stand back!

(eine Stimme)
Zurück!

The First Priest appears.

Mortal! You have deserved to wander forever
in the gloomy abysses of the earth.
But the gentle gods have remitted that punishment.
However, you shall never experience the
exalted pleasure of the Brotherhood.

Mensch! Du hättest verdient, auf immer
in düsteren Klüften der Erde zu wandern.
Die gütigen Götter entlassen dich der Strafe.
Dafür aber wirst du das himmlische
Vergnügen der Eingeweihten nie fühlen.

Have you no other earthly desire?

Und sonst hast du keinen Wunsch in dieser Welt?

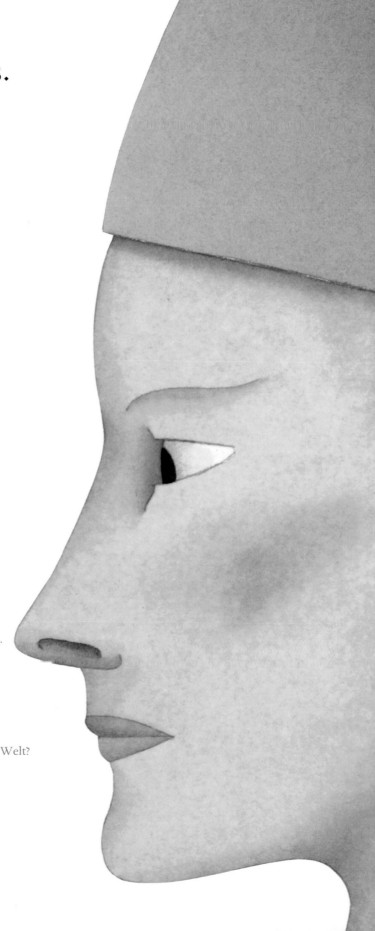

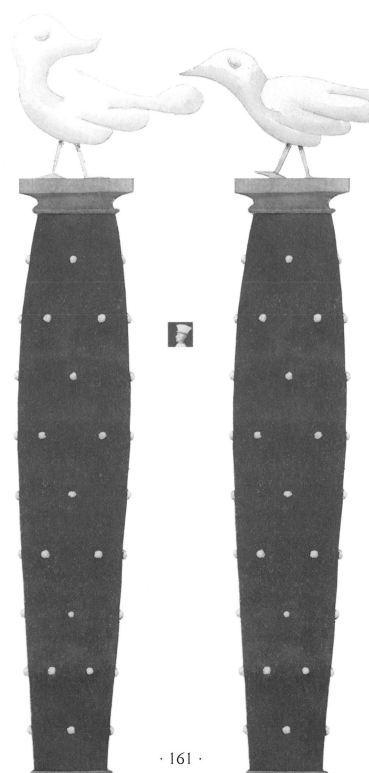

Ein Mädchen oder Weibchen
Wünscht Papageno sich.
O, so ein sanftes Täubchen
Wär' Seligkeit für mich!
Dann schmeckte mir Trinken und Essen,
Dann könnt' mit Fürsten mich messen,
Des Lebens als Weiser mich freun,
Und wie im Elysium sein.

Ein Mädchen oder Weibchen
Wünscht Papageno sich.
O, so ein sanftes Täubchen
Wär' Seligkeit für mich!
Ach, kann ich denn keiner von allen
Den reizenden Mädchen gefallen?
Helf' eine mir nur aus der Not,
Sonst gräm' ich mich wahrlich zu Tod.

Ein Mädchen oder Weibchen
Wünscht Papageno sich.
O, so ein sanftes Täubchen
Wär' Seligkeit für mich!
Wird keine mir Liebe gewähren,
So muß mich die Flamme verzehren!
Doch küsst' mich ein weiblicher Mund,
So bin ich schon wieder gesund!

A sweetheart or a bride
Is Papageno's wish.
A cute and curvy, moon-eyed
Turtledove's his dish!
With food to sate and wine to rinse,
I'd be the equal of any prince.
That's all the wisdom I'd ever need.
There's my heaven, yes indeed!

A sweetheart or a bride
Is Papageno's wish.
A cute and curvy, moon-eyed
Turtledove's his dish!
So many girls flutter around me.
Not a single one as yet has found me.
With no one to love me, no one to care,
I'm driven into the arms of despair!

A sweetheart or a bride
Is Papageno's wish.
A cute and curvy, moon-eyed
Turtledove's his dish!
If just one kiss is longer denied,
I'll die of this burning fever inside!
All I need is just that kiss
To put me in a twittering bliss.

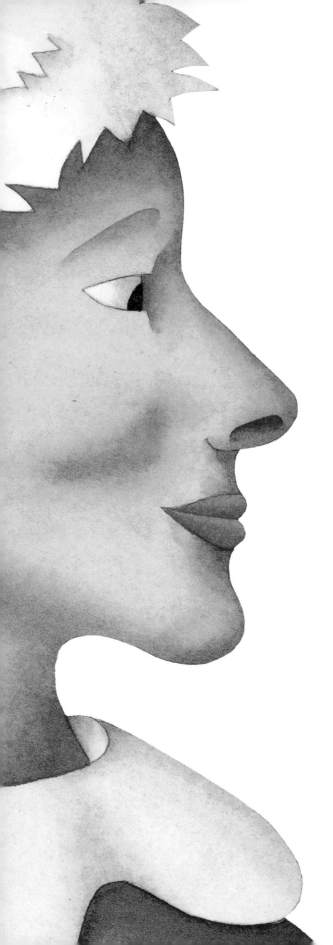

TWENTY·THIRD SCENE

Da bin ich schon, mein Engel!	Here I am, my angel!
Ja, mein Engel!	I have, my angel!
Und wenn du mir versprichst, mir ewig treu zu bleiben, dann sollst du sehen, wie zärtlich dein Weibchen dich lieben wird.	And if you promise to be true to me forever, you will see how tenderly your little wife will love you.
Papageno, ich rate dir, zaudre nicht! Deine Hand, sonst bist du hier auf immer eingekerkert.	Papageno, I'd advise you not to hesitate. Give me your hand, or you'll be imprisoned here forever.
Ohne Freundin mußt du leben und der Welt auf immer entsagen.	And have to live without a sweetheart and renounce the world forever.
Das schwörst du?	Do you swear it?
(verwandelt sich in ein junges Weib, welches ebenso gekleidet ist, wie Papageno) Papageno!	*(turning into a young woman dressed exactly like Papageno)* Papageno!

TWENTY·FOURTH SCENE

Fort mit dir, junges Weib! Er ist deiner noch nicht würdig! Papageno, zurück!	Away with you, young woman! He is not yet worthy of you. Papageno, stand back!

An old woman enters, dancing and leaning on her stick.

So you took pity on me?	Du hast dich meiner erbarmt?
That's lucky!	Das ist ein Glück!
Not so fast, dear heart. With marriage, a man needs time to think things over.	Nur nicht so hastig, lieber Engel! So ein Bündnis braucht doch seine Überlegung.
Imprisoned?	Eingekerkert?
Renounce the world? No, better an old wife than no wife. So here is my hand on it. I will always be true to you . . . *(aside)* . . . until I see a prettier bird!	Der Welt entsagen?—Nein, da will ich doch lieber die Alte nehmen, als gar keine. Nun, da hast du meine Hand darauf, daß ich dir immer getreu bleibe . . . *(für sich)* . . . solang ich keine Schönere finde.
Yes, I swear it!	Ja, das schwör' ich!
Papagena! *(He rushes forward to embrace her.)*	Papagena! *(Er will sie umarmen.)*

The First Priest appears.

The earth would have to open its jaws and swallow me, before I'd ever withdraw. *(The earth begins to tremble. He sinks to the ground.)* O gods, I'm sinking!	Eh' ich mich zurückziehe, soll die Erde mich verschlingen. *(Er sinkt hinab.)* Ihr Götter! Ich versinke!

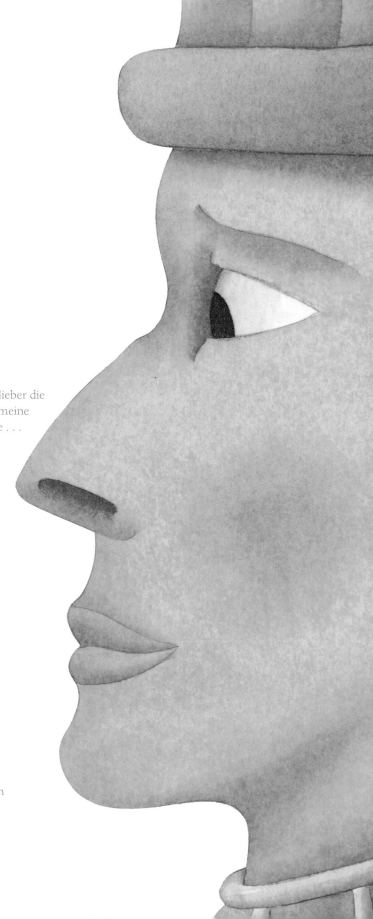

TWENTY-FIFTH SCENE

A garden at dawn.
The Three Spirits are
watching over Pamina
from a distance.

Bald prangt, den Morgen zu verkünden,
　　Die Sonn' auf goldner Bahn!
Bald soll der Aberglaube schwinden,
　　Bald siegt der weise Mann.
　　O holde Ruhe, steig hernieder,
Kehr in der Menschen Herzen wieder;
　　Dann ist die Erd' ein Himmelreich,
　　Und Sterbliche den Göttern gleich.

 Soon the glorious sun will take
Its golden course across the sky!
The foes of superstition wake
And wisdom is enthroned on high.
Soon peace will bring its remedies.
Enlightenment will bless the wise.
Then mankind will be truly free
And earth become a paradise!

Doch seht, Verzweiflung quält Pamina.

 But see, despair torments Pamina.

　　　　Wo ist sie denn?

Where is she then?

　　　Sie ist von Sinnen.

 She's out of her senses.

Sie quält verschmähter Liebe Leiden.
Laßt uns der Armen Trost bereiten!
Fürwahr, ihr Schicksal geht uns nah!
　　O wäre nur ihr Jüngling da!
Sie kommt, laßt uns beiseite gehn,
Damit wir, was sie mache, sehn.
　　　　(Sie gehen beiseite.)

She feels the pang of love's rejection,
So let us grant her our protection.
To her fortunes we all feel near—
If only her young Prince were here!
She comes, so let us stay unseen
And wait to learn what this may mean.
(They withdraw.)

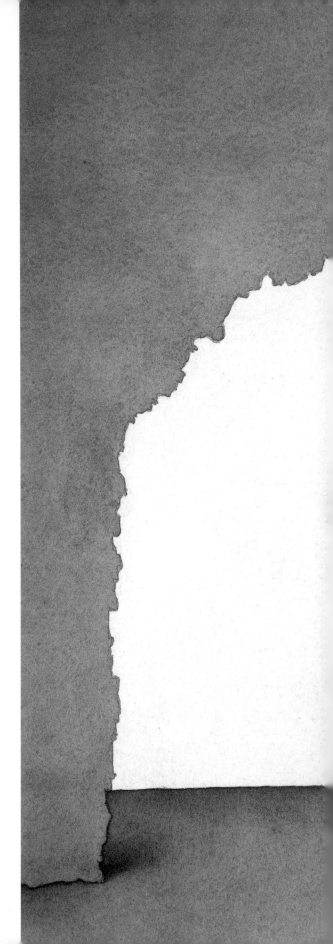

TWENTY-SIXTH SCENE

With the Three
Spirits hidden,
Pamina enters half-
crazed, a dagger in
her hand.

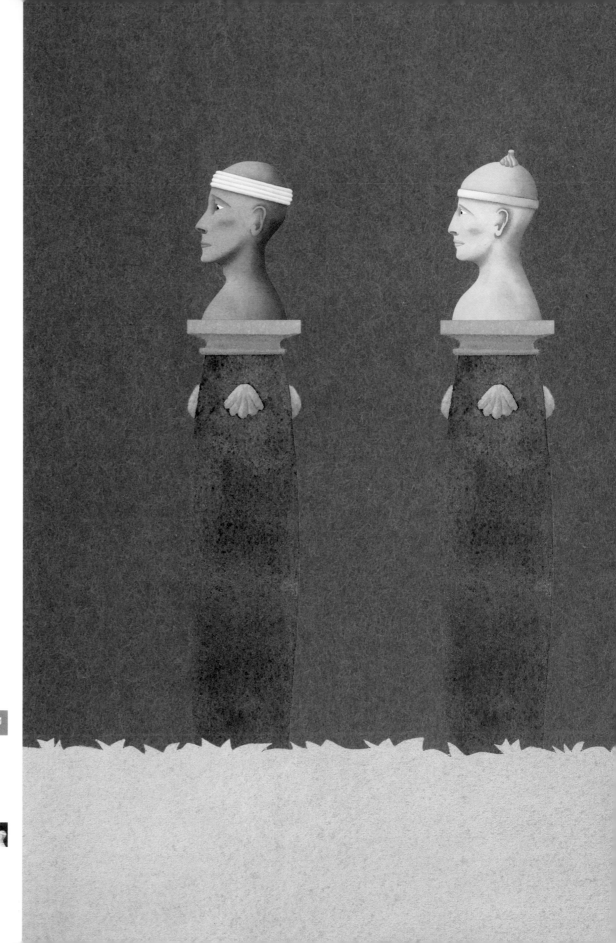

(to the dagger)
This blade's the groom I now must wed.
The grave will be my marriage bed.

(zum Dolch)
Du also bist mein Bräutigam?
Durch dich vollend' ich meinen Gram.

(aside)
What gloomy words to overhear.
The poor girl's madness must be near.
(beiseite)
Welch' dunkle Worte sprach sie da?
Die Arme ist dem Wahnsinn nah.

Geduld, mein Trauter, ich bin dein,	Be calm, beloved, I belong to you.
Bald werden wir vermählet sein.	What grief your kiss will now undo!
Wahnsinn tobt ihr im Gehirne;	Surely frenzy clouds her brain.
Selbstmord steht auf ihrer Stirne.	How would suicide end her pain?
Holdes Mädchen, sieh uns an!	Dearest maiden, look! Over here!
Sterben will ich, weil der Mann,	Death is certain. Now all is clear.
Den ich nimmermehr kann hassen,	The husband who could never hurt me
Seine Traute kann verlassen.	Has cruelly chosen to desert me.
(auf den Dolch zeigend)	*(pointing to the dagger)*
Dies gab meine Mutter mir.	This friend my mother gave to me.
Selbstmord strafet Gott an dir.	The gods forbid this by decree!
Lieber durch dies Eisen sterben,	Better by this blade to die
Als durch Liebesgram verderben.	Than linger with a loveless lie.
Mutter, durch dich leide ich,	Mother, mother, it is your curse
Und dein Fluch verfolget mich.	That forces me to do the worst.
Mädchen, willst du mit uns gehn?	Maiden, come away with us!
Ja, des Jammers Maß ist voll!	My grief is now too much to tell.
Falscher Jüngling, lebe wohl!	False Tamino, farewell, farewell!
Sieh, Pamina stirbt durch dich:	See how for you Pamina dies.
Dieses Eisen töte mich.	This dagger stops the tears and sighs.
Ha, Unglückliche! Halt ein!	Stop! Poor girl, so sad and lonely!
Sollte dies dein Jüngling sehen,	If Tamino could be near you,
Würde er vor Gram vergehen;	He would surely weep to hear you.
Denn er liebet dich allein.	The Prince loves you and you only.
Was? Er fühlte Gegenliebe?	You say he loved me in return,
Und verbarg mir seine Triebe,	Pretending so to scoff and spurn?
Wandte sein Gesicht von mir?	Is it one's beloved one betrays?
Warum sprach er nicht mit mir?	For me alone he could not stay?
Dieses müssen wir verschweigen,	To tell you that is not allowed,
Doch wir wollen dir ihn zeigen!	Though we may lead you to him now.
Und du wirst mit Staunen sehn,	Follow us and you will see
Dass er dir sein Herz geweiht,	His devotion and his bravery.
Und den Tod für dich nicht scheut.	Death itself he dares somehow!
Führt mich hin, ich möcht' ihn sehen!	Lead me to him! I long to see!
Komm, wir wollen zu ihm gehen.	Follow us and you will see.
Zwei Herzen, die von Liebe brennen	*All* Two hearts that beat as one forever
Kann Menschenohnmacht niemals trennen.	Not even doubt and weakness sever.
Verloren ist der Feinde Müh',	Their enemies may plot elsewhere,
Die Götter selbst beschützen sie.	But the gods protect this noble pair.

TWENTY-SEVENTH SCENE

Giant mountains tower.
Two Men in Armor
lead Tamino in.

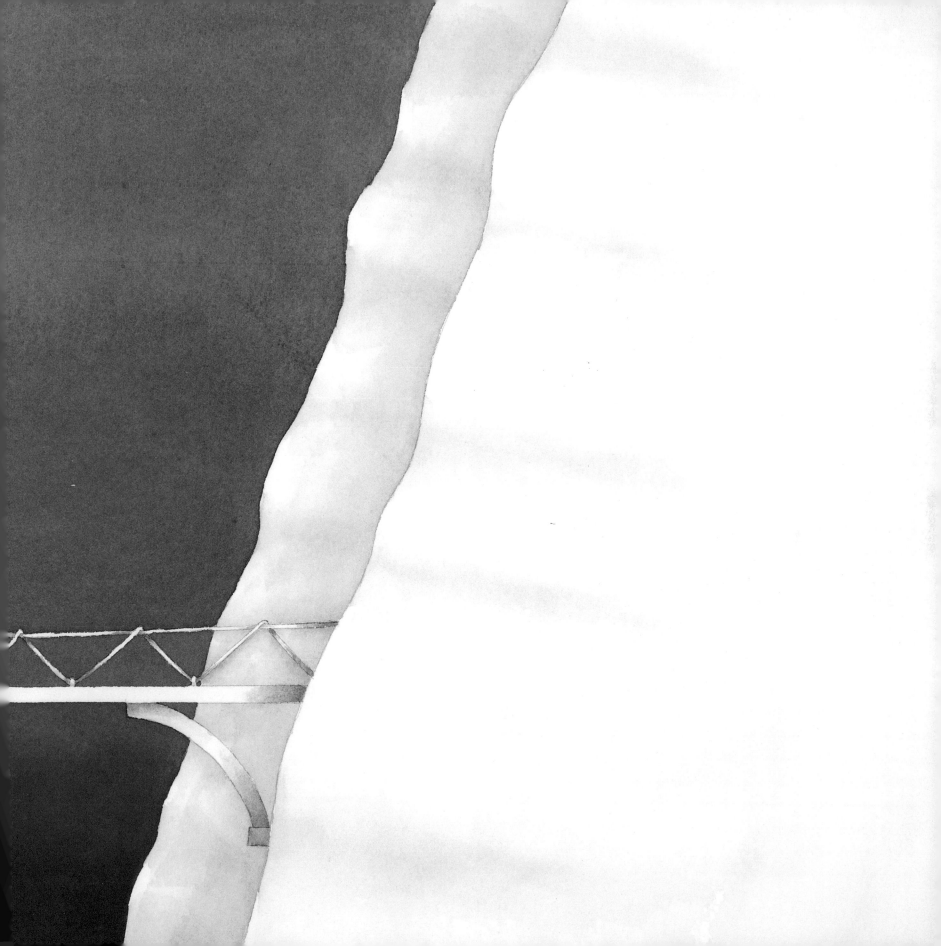

He who walks this path of trials,
By fire, water, air, and earth is tested.
If he can conquer fear of death,
He will rise from earth to heaven.
Enlightened, he will understand
All the mysteries of Isis.

Der, welcher wandert diese Straße voll Beschwerden,
Wird rein durch Feuer, Wasser, Luft und Erden;
Wenn er des Todes Schrecken überwinden kann,
Schwingt er sich aus der Erde himmelan.
Erleuchtet wird er dann imstande sein,
Sich den Mysterien der Isis ganz zu weihn.

Death I defy, and like a man
Keep on the journey I began.
Unlock the fatal gates of fear—
Virtue leads me, the way is clear.
(He is about to enter.)

Mich schreckt kein Tod, als Mann zu handeln,
Den Weg der Tugend fortzuwandeln.
Schließt mir die Schreckenspforten auf,
Ich wage froh den kühnen Lauf.
(will gehen)

(from afar)
Tamino, wait! I must see you!
(von innen)
Tamino, halt! Ich muß dich sehn.

What was that? Pamina's voice!
Was hör' ich! Paminens Stimme?

Yes, that was Pamina's voice.
Ja, ja, das ist Paminens Stimme.

What joy if she is at my side!
No destiny can separate us,
Though death itself at last await us!
Wohl mir, nun kann sie mit mir gehn,
Nun trennet uns kein Schicksal mehr,
Wenn auch der Tod beschieden wär'!

· 176 ·

What joy if she be at his side!
No destiny can separate them,
Though death itself at last await them!
Wohl dir, nun kann sie mit dir gehn,
Nun trennet euch kein Schicksal mehr,
Wenn auch der Tod beschieden wär'!

Am I allowed to break my silence?
Ist mir erlaubt, mit ihr zu sprechen?

You are allowed to break your silence.
Dir ist erlaubt, mit ihr zu sprechen!

What joy when we can meet again!
Welch Glück, wenn wir uns wiedersehn,

What joy when they can meet again!
Welch Glück, wenn wir euch wiedersehn.

To enter the Temple hand in hand!
The woman who braves the deadly night
Is worthy to receive the light.
(Pamina is led in by the Second Priest.)
Froh Hand in Hand in Tempel gehn.
Ein Weib, das Nacht und Tod nicht scheut,
Ist würdig und wird eingeweiht.
(Pamina wird vom zweiten Priester hereingeführt.)

Oh Tamino! My love! My joy!
Tamino mein! O welch ein Glück!

Oh Pamina! My love! My joy!
Behold the gates of terror
Where death and destiny loom.
Pamina mein, o welch ein Glück!
Hier sind die Schreckenspforten,
Die Not und Tod mir dräuen.

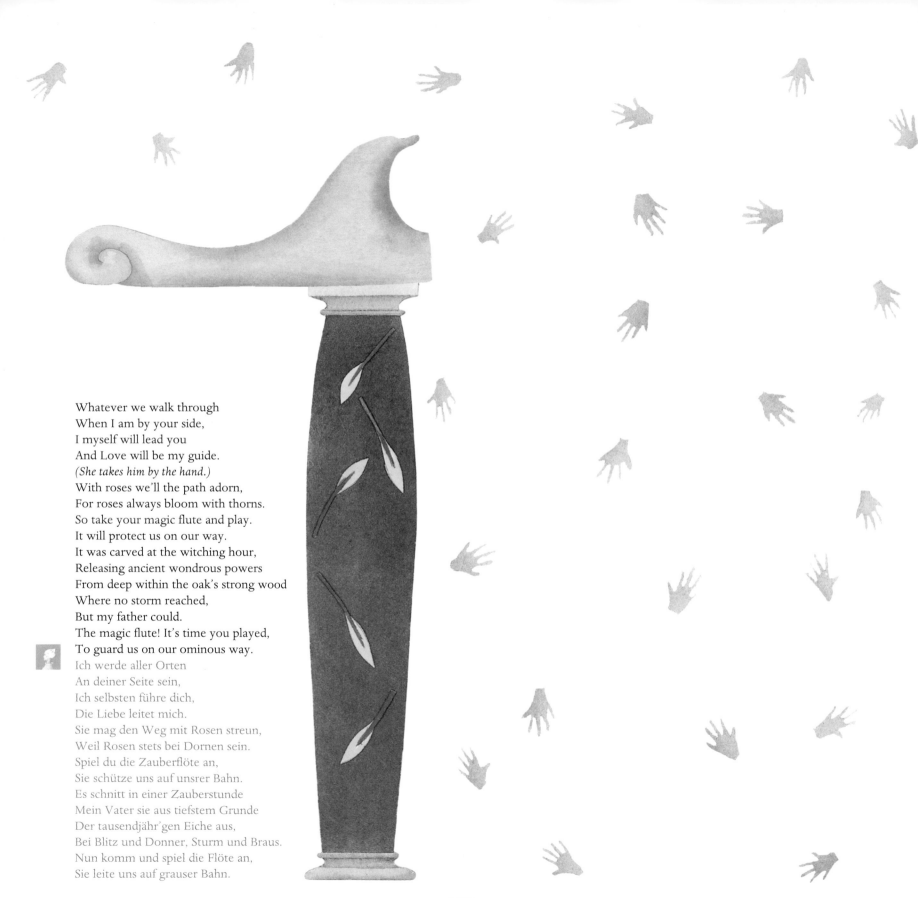

Whatever we walk through
When I am by your side,
I myself will lead you
And Love will be my guide.
(She takes him by the hand.)
With roses we'll the path adorn,
For roses always bloom with thorns.
So take your magic flute and play.
It will protect us on our way.
It was carved at the witching hour,
Releasing ancient wondrous powers
From deep within the oak's strong wood
Where no storm reached,
But my father could.
The magic flute! It's time you played,
To guard us on our ominous way.

Ich werde aller Orten
An deiner Seite sein,
Ich selbsten führe dich,
Die Liebe leitet mich.
Sie mag den Weg mit Rosen streun,
Weil Rosen stets bei Dornen sein.
Spiel du die Zauberflöte an,
Sie schütze uns auf unsrer Bahn.
Es schnitt in einer Zauberstunde
Mein Vater sie aus tiefstem Grunde
Der tausendjähr'gen Eiche aus,
Bei Blitz und Donner, Sturm und Braus.
Nun komm und spiel die Flöte an,
Sie leite uns auf grauser Bahn.

· 178 ·

Encircled with sweet music's might
We walk into death's darkest night.
Wir wandeln durch des Tones Macht,
Froh durch des Todes düstre Nacht!

Encircled with sweet music's might
They walk into death's darkest night.
Ihr wandelt durch des Tones Macht,
Froh durch des Todes düstre Nacht.

(They pass through the caves
of fire and water.)
We've traveled through
the blazing furnace,
And withstood its fiery grave.
Now to try the watery menace,
Again with hope the flute will save.
(Sie durchwandeln eine Feuerhöhle
und eine Wasserhöhle.)
Wir wandelten durch Feuersgluten,
Bekämpften mutig die Gefahr.
Dein Ton sei Schütz in Wasserfluten,
So wie er es im Feuer war.

Our triumph the all-wise gods allow!
The mighty Isis stands by us now!
Ihr Götter! Welch ein Augenblick!
Gewähret ist uns Isis' Glück.

(von innen)
Triumph! Triumph! Du edles Paar!
Besieget hast du die Gefahr,
Der Isis Weihe ist nun dein,
Kommt, tretet in den Tempel ein!
(Sie werden in den Tempel geführt.)

(from within)
Rejoice! Rejoice! You valiant pair!
You have emerged from danger's lair.
Isis has smiled on your noble minds.
Come, enter now our Temple's shrine!
(They are led into the Temple.)

TWENTY-EIGHTH SCENE
A garden. Papageno enters, with a rope.

(ruft mit seinem Pfeifchen)
Papagena, Papagena, Papagena!
Weibchen, Täubchen, meine Schöne!
Vergebens! Ach, sie ist verloren!
Ich bin zum Unglück schon geboren.
Ich plauderte, und das war schlecht,
Und drum geschieht es mir schon recht.
Seit ich gekostet diesen Wein,
Seit ich das schöne Weibchen sah,
So brennt's im Herzenskämmerlein,
So zwickt es hier, so zwickt es da.
Papagena, Herzensweibchen!
Papagena, liebes Täubchen!
'S ist umsonst, es ist vergebens!
Müde bin ich meines Lebens!
Sterben macht der Lieb' ein End',
Wenn's im Herzen noch so brennt.
(nimmt einen Strick)
Diesen Baum da will ich zieren,
Mir an ihm den Hals zuschnüren,
Weil das Leben mir mißfällt;
Gute Nacht, du falsche Welt.
Weil du böse an mir handelst,
Mir kein schönes Kind zubandelst,
So ist's aus, so sterbe ich.
Schöne Mädchen, denkt an mich.
Will sich eine um mich Armen,
Eh' ich hänge, noch erbarmen,
Wohl, so laß ich's diesmal sein!
Rufet nur: ja, oder nein!
Keine hört mich, alles stille!
Also ist es euer Wille?
Papageno, frisch hinauf!
Ende deinen Lebenslauf.
Nun, ich warte noch, es sei,
Bis man zählet eins, zwei, drei.
(pfeift)
Eins!
Zwei! Halb drei!
Drei!
Nun wohlan, es bleibt dabei!
Weil mich nichts zurücke hält;
Gute Nacht, du falsche Welt.
(Er will sich hängen.)

 (playing on his panpipe)
Papagena, Papagena, Papagena!
Sweetheart! Dearest! My beloved!
Useless! She is lost forever!
I was never meant to have her.
By chattering I missed my chance.
Here's the end to my romance.
Ever since I sipped that wine
And saw the girl that should be mine,
The fire in my heart's severe.
It warms me there, and scorches here!
Papagena! My dove! My darling!
Papagena! My pretty starling!
She doesn't know the way to find me.
It's time to leave the world behind me.
Since my love was all in vain,
It's time to end a life of pain.
(He takes his rope.)
I'd decorate this sturdy tree
With the hanging body of . . . me.
My wretched life has been misspent.
Goodbye, world. You won't lament.
All you did was to mistreat me,
And now no little wife to greet me.
So this is it. It's time to die.
Pretty maidens, goodbye! Goodbye!
If there were just someone to care,
Take pity on me, want to spare—
Yes! this once I might relent!
Speak up! Have I your consent?
No one hears me. No reply.
Well, I guess I'll have to die.
Come on, Papageno, the rope—
Can't you see there is no hope.
Wait! One more chance. Let's see.
Suppose I count from one to three . . .
(He plays his pipe, looking around.)
One!
Two! . . . Two . . . and a half!
Three.
Not a sound. The die is cast!
No sympathy? No help? All right!
You unlucky world of pain, goodnight!
(He starts to hang himself.)

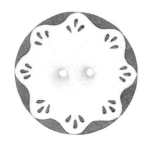

Halt ein, o Papageno, und sei klug;
Man lebt nur einmal, dies sei dir genug.

 Papageno! Wait! Take our advice.
You live just once. Let that suffice.

Ihr habt gut reden, habt gut scherzen;
Doch brennt' es euch wie mich im Herzen,
Ihr würdet auch nach Mädchen gehn.

Wise advice. Go on, mock me!
If, like me, your hearts were aswirl,
You too would be chasing after girls.

So lasse deine Glöckchen klingen,
Dies wird dein Weibchen zu dir bringen.

Take up your magic bells and play.
Your sweetheart will soon enough obey.

Ich Narr vergaß der Zauberdinge!
Erklinge, Glockenspiel, erklinge!
Ich muß mein liebes Mädchen sehn.
Klinget, Glöckchen, klinget,
Schafft mein Mädchen her!
Klinget, Glöckchen, klinget,
Bringt mein Weibchen her!

What a fool! I forgot the bells!
My pretty chimes, come cast your spell!
You'll bring her back as nothing will.
Ring, little bells, ring out,
Bring my sweetheart here!
Ring, little bells, ring out,
Bring my sweetheart dear!

Nun, Papageno, sieh dich um!

Now, Papageno, look around!

Pa-Pa-Pa-Pa-Pa-Pa-Papagena!

Pa-Pa-Pa-Pa-Pa-Pa-Papagena!

Pa-Pa-Pa-Pa-Pa-Pa-Papageno!

Pa-Pa-Pa-Pa-Pa-Pa-Papageno!

Bist du mir nun ganz gegeben?

Now will you be mine forever?

Nun bin ich dir ganz gegeben. Now I will be yours forever!

Nun, so sei mein liebes Weibchen! Now you'll be my little love!

Nun, so sei mein Herzenstäubchen! Now you'll be my turtledove!

Welche Freude wird das sein! Oh, what bliss! Oh, what joy!
Wenn die Götter uns bedenken, May the gods bless us
Unsrer Liebe Kinder schenken, And crown our caresses
So liebe kleine Kinderlein! With many a little girl and boy!

Erst einen kleinen Papageno! First a little Papageno!

Dann eine kleine Papagena! Then a little Papagena!

Dann wieder einen Papageno! Then another Papageno!

Dann wieder eine Papagena! Then another Papagena!

Papagena! Papageno! Papagenas! Papagenos!
Es ist das höchste der Gefühle, The greatest joy of any
Wenn viele viele Is many, many
Pa-Pa-Pa-Pa-geno, Pa-Pa-Pa-Papagenos,
Pa-Pa-Pa-Pa-gena, Pa-Pa-Pa-Papagenas.
Der Eltern Segen werden sein. To bless their parents' nest!
(beide ab) *(They rush off giddily.)*

TWENTY-NINTH SCENE

A vault inside the
mountain. Monostatos
is with the Queen
of the Night and
the Three Ladies.

Softly, softly, one step more!
We'll soon be at the Temple door.
Nur stille, stille, stille, stille!
Bald dringen wir im Tempel ein.

Softly, softly, one step more!
We'll soon be at the Temple door.

Nur stille, stille, stille, stille!
Bald dringen wir im Tempel ein.

Your Highness, I pray you keep your word—
You promised your child as my bride.
Doch Fürstin, halte Wort! Erfülle—
Dein Kind muß meine Gattin sein.

That is my will. I'll keep my word.
I promised my child as your bride.
Ich halte Wort; es ist mein Wille.
Mein Kind soll deine Gattin sein.

She promised her child as your bride.
Ihr Kind soll deine Gattin sein.

Silence! I hear a roaring sound.
Like thunder, or a waterfall.
Doch still! Ich höre schrecklich rauschen,
Wie Donnerton und Wasserfall.

Yes, that roaring is a frightful sound,
Like distant thunder's threatening call.
Ja, fürchterlich ist dieses Rauschen
Wie fernen Donners Widerhall.

Now they are in the Temple's hall.
Nun sind sie in des Tempels Hallen.

And now is when the lightning falls!
Our flaming swords for the enemy!
We will destroy their blasphemy!   *All*
Dort wollen wir sie überfallen,
Die Frömmler tilgen von der Erd'
Mit Feuersglut und mächt'gem Schwert.

Glorious Queen, accept this fight
As your last sacrificial rite!
Dir, große Königin der Nacht,
Sei unsrer Rache Opfer gebracht.

(thunder, lightning, wind)
(Donner, Blitz, Sturm)

Shattered, ruined is our might,
All plunged into endless night!   *All*
Zerschmettert, vernichtet ist unsere Macht,
Wir alle gestürzet in ewige Nacht.

(Suddenly the whole scene is transformed
into a blaze of sunlight.)
(Sogleich verwandelt sich das ganze
Theater in eine Sonne.)

THIRTIETH SCENE

The Temple of the Sun. Sarastro stands
on high. Tamino and Pamina are dressed
in priestly garments before him. The Priests
and the Three Spirits stand by them.

The sun's golden splendor has banished the night,
The forces of evil been vanquished by right.

Die Strahlen der Sonne vertreiben die Nacht,
Vernichten der Heuchler erschlichene Macht.

Alle

Heil sei euch Geweihten! Ihr dranget durch Nacht,
Dank sei dir Osiris, Dank dir, Isis, gebracht!
Es siegte die Stärke und krönet zum Lohn
Die Schönheit und Weisheit mit ewiger Kron'!

All

Hail to those who have passed through the night!
By Osiris and Isis brought to the light!
Brave hearts have won the glorious crown!
May Beauty to Wisdom forever be bound!

Editors: Nancy Grubb and Russell Stockman
Typography: Patricia Fabricant
Production Manager: Louise Kurtz

First edition
2 4 6 8 10 9 7 5 3 1

Library of Congress Cataloging-in-Publication Data

Mozart, Wolfgang Amadeus, 1756–1791.
[Zauberflöte. Libretto. English]
The magic flute / music by Wolfgang Amadeus Mozart; libretto by Emanuel Schikaneder; [illustrated by] Davide Pizzigoni; translated by J. D. McClatchy.
p. cm.
ISBN 0-7892-0645-5 (alk. paper)
1. Operas—Librettos. I. Schikaneder, Emanuel, 1751–1812. II. Pizzigoni, Davide.
III. McClatchy, J. D., 1945– IV. Title.
ML50.M939 Z32 2000
782.1'0268—dc21
00-025259

ACKNOWLEDGMENTS

Davide Pizzigoni is indebted to Ivan
Fornaroli and Elisabetta Ozino Calligaris
for their help and advice.

J. D. McClatchy is grateful to the
Bogliasco Foundation for a residency
at the Centro Studi Ligure, where this
translation was made.

PERFORMANCE NOTES

JONATHAN ROMEO

The Magic Flute (Die Zauberflöte) is the product of a unique collaboration between the actor-manager Emanuel Schikaneder, who commissioned it in 1791, and the composer Wolfgang Amadeus Mozart—who at age thirty-five was at the height of his creative genius and in the last year of his tragically short life. It is a German Singspiel (sung/spoken) opera in two acts, with a libretto attributed to Schikaneder, though it was probably written mostly by C. L. Giesecke, an actor in Schikaneder's company.

Mozart began working on the score in March of 1791, and it premiered in Vienna on September 30 of the same year. The speed of this accomplishment is especially astonishing when one considers that Mozart also traveled to Prague during this period to write *La Clemenza di Tito* for the coronation of Emperor Leopold II as King of Bohemia and began composing his *Requiem*. Schikaneder's production was performed over one hundred times and toured in every country in Europe except Italy. Today, *The Magic Flute* remains one of the most performed operas in the international repertory.

On July 30, 1937, the Italian conductor Arturo Toscanini conducted the Vienna Philharmonic Orchestra with the Vienna State Opera Chorus in a performance of *The Magic Flute* at the Salzburg Festival, in Austria. The two compact disks included here contain an original live recording of that performance, newly remastered with state-of-the-art technology. The production featured Helge Roswaenge as Tamino, Willi Domgraf-Faßbaender as Papageno, Alexander Kipnis as Sarastro, Jarmila Novotná as Pamina, Julie Osváth as The Queen of the Night, and William Wernigk as Monostatos. The keyboard glockenspiel heard as Papageno's bells was played by the young George Solti (later to become one of the world's most prominent conductors), who was Toscanini's assistant for this production.

Well known for his fiery spirit, the seventy-year-old Toscanini conducted at a rapid pace that becomes evident in the opening notes of the overture's allegro section. His extensive rehearsal periods were grueling, and the quick tempos demanded by the tireless conductor pushed the singers to their limits. When the singers finally put their manager up to the task of addressing their complaints to the maestro in his dressing room, Toscanini quietly retorted, "I thought you were all interested in the opera as much as I am." Sadly, this was Toscanini's last season at the Salzburg Festival. He resigned on February 16, 1938, in protest against the German occupation of Austria.

CAST

Arturo Toscanini, CONDUCTOR

Vienna Philharmonic Orchestra
with the Vienna State Opera Chorus

SARASTRO	Alexander Kipnis
TAMINO	Helge Roswaenge
THE SPEAKER	Alfred Jerger
THE QUEEN OF THE NIGHT	Julie Osváth
PAMINA	Jarmila Novotná
PAPAGENO	Willi Domgraf-Faßbaender
PAPAGENA	Dora Komarek
MONOSTATOS	William Wernigk
FIRST SPIRIT	Kurt Pech
SECOND SPIRIT	Albert Feuhl
THIRD SPIRIT	Fritz Mascha
FIRST LADY	Hilde Konetzni
SECOND LADY	Stefania Fratnikova
THIRD LADY	Kerstin Thorborg
FIRST MAN IN ARMOR	Anton Dermota
SECOND MAN IN AAN IN	Carl Bissuti
OLD PRIEST	Richard Sallaba

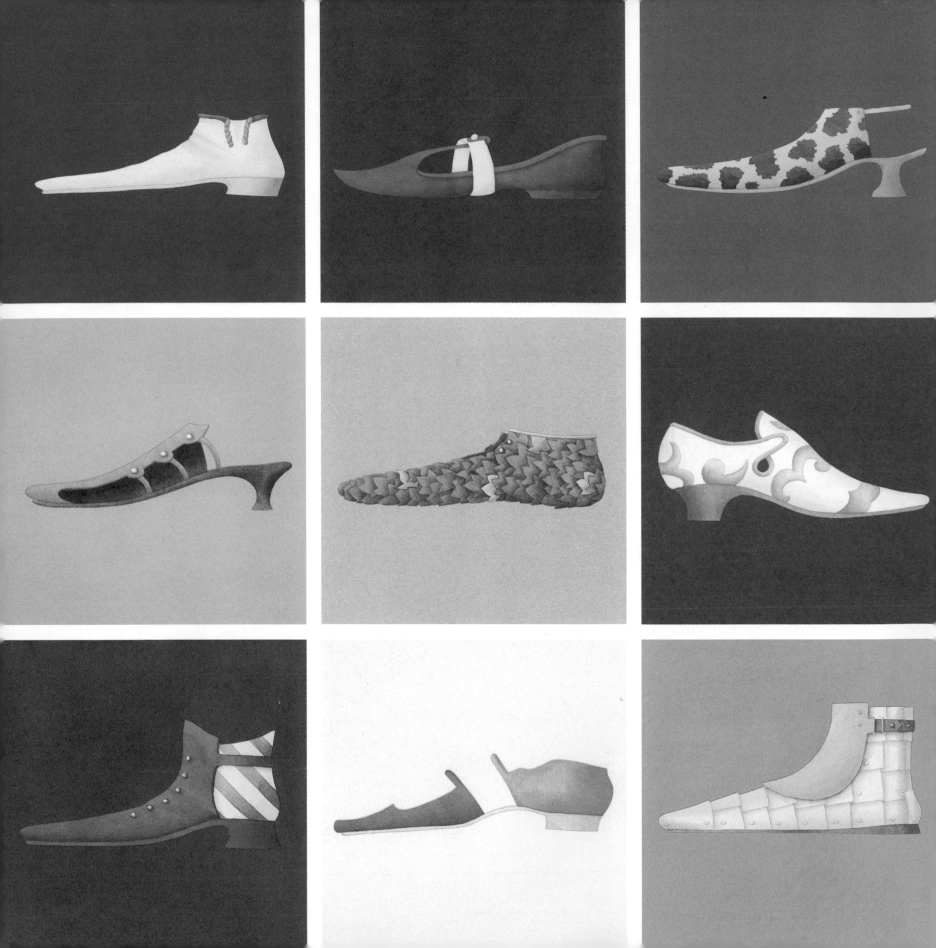